Domenico Speranza

**Songs for Catholic Schools and the Catechism in Rhyme**

With original music

Domenico Speranza

**Songs for Catholic Schools and the Catechism in Rhyme**
*With original music*

ISBN/EAN: 9783337394462

Printed in Europe, USA, Canada, Australia, Japan

Cover: Foto ©Lupo / pixelio.de

More available books at **www.hansebooks.com**

# SONGS

## FOR

# CATHOLIC SCHOOLS,

## AND

## THE CATECHISM IN RHYME.

### BY

### REV. DR. CUMMINGS,
Pastor of St. Stephen's Church, New York.

WITH ORIGINAL MUSIC.

NEW YORK:
D. & J. SADLIER,
31 BARCLAY STREET.

## TO THE PUBLIC.

The Art of Music in our day has assumed an importance in Schools not claimed for it heretofore. From being an accessory and ornamental branch of education, it has risen to the dignity of a powerful means for conveying instruction, assisting the memory, and ennobling the heart, and it is daily resorted to with success as an effective engine for enforcing discipline, and preserving order. It is thus instrumental in organizing and marshalling large bodies of scholars as well as in entertaining and refining them.

As an important auxiliary in religious instruction and worship it has been prized by all men, but never more highly than by the members of the Catholic Church. The "Songs for Catholic Schools" have passed through several editions, and steadily increased in popularity ever since their first appearance, as eminently well fitted to subserve the varied objects to which we have referred.

The undersigned are happy to announce that they have secured the exclusive right of publishing the work, and to offer their patrons and friends this edition as the fullest and most correct which has appeared up to the present time.

D. & J. SADLIER.

# PREFACE.

I RESPECTFULLY ask of the Catholic public a fair trial for this collection of melodies, prepared at the urgent request of Bishops and Clergymen in every part of the United States. It bears the title of "Songs for Catholic Schools," being chiefly designed for singing or recitation in Sunday-schools and day-schools under Catholic direction, but it will be found useful also by church choirs, religious communities, and private families. It is the first original collection of the kind ever published in this country. This fact, it is hoped, will excuse its imperfections, and at the same time obtain for it a friendly reception on the part of all who have at heart the religious improvement of American Catholic children.

The " Definitions and Aids to Memory," in the second part of the book, are a brief catechism in rhyme, a plan of conveying religious instruction which has been tried with excellent results among young and illiterate persons in other countries. The singing or chanting of such rhymes causes them to be learned quicker, and impresses them more deeply on the memory. We have, therefore, set to music the portions best adapted for the purpose.

The getting up of such a work involves a vast amount of labor, care, and expense; that it may go forth with God's blessing and do some good, is the earnest prayer of its author.

J. W. CUMMINGS.

St. Stephen's Church, New York.

# CONTENTS.

| | PAGE | MUSIC NOS. |
|---|---|---|
| Hymn to St. Stephen | 5 | 1 |
| The Music of Nature | 7 | 2 |
| The Messenger Angel | 8 | 3 |
| Morning Prayer | 11 | 4 |
| Hail! Virgin of Virgins | 12 | 5 |
| The Invocation | 14 | 6 |
| The Church | 17 | 7 |
| The Ascension | 19 | 8 |
| The Blessing | 21 | 9 |
| Prayer against Temptation | 22 | 10 |
| Holy Communion | 24 | 11 |
| The Annunciation | 25 | 12 |
| The Sleep of the Infant Jesus | 26 | 13 |
| Hymn to Mary | 29 | 14 |
| A Child's May Song | 30 | 15 |
| The Tear of Innocence | 32 | 16 |
| Purgatory | 33 | 17 |
| A Night Prayer | 34 | 18 |
| Song of the Union | 35 | 19 |
| The Blessed Eucharist | 36 | 20 |
| Child's Hymn to the Guardian Angel | 38 | 21 |
| Hymn of the Crusaders | 40 | 23, 25 |
| Hymn of the Hebrews | 41 | 22, 24 |
| Recollection | 42 | 23, 25 |
| Encouragement | 42 | 22, 24 |
| Hymn to the Blessed Trinity | 43 | 26 |
| " to the Holy Ghost | 44 | 27 |
| " of Praise | 46 | 28 |
| " of Trust | 48 | 29 |
| " of Thanksgiving | 50 | 30 |
| " of Hope | 53 | 31 |
| " for Communion of Children | 55 | 32 |
| " to St. Joseph | 57 | 33 |

## CONTENTS.

|  | PAGE. | MUSIC NOS. |
|---|---|---|
| Hymn to St. Francis de Sales | 59 | 34 |
| " to St. Jane Frances de Chantal | 61 | 35 |
| " to St. Vincent de Paul | 62 | 36 |
| " to St. Mary Magdalen | 64 | 37 |
| " to St. Teresa | 65 | 38 |
| " to Mary, Help of Christians | 67 | 39 |
| " for the Month of Mary | 68 | 40 |
| The Lord's Day | 70 | 41 |
| The Child Jesus | 72 | 42 |
| The Seven Archangels | 74 | 43 |
| Mass Hymn | 75 | 44 |
| God Save the Commonwealth | 78 | 45 |
| The Holy Innocents | 79 | 46 |
| Dew-Drops of Wisdom | 80 | 47 |
| The Language of Feeling | 84 | 48 |
| The Voyage of Life | 85 | 49 |
| Death | 86 | 50 |
| The Angel and the Child | 87 | 55 |
| The Virtues at Bethlehem | 89 | 56 |
| The Hour of Prayer | 90 | 57 |
| Queen of Angels | 92 | 58 |
| Salutation to Mary | 94 | 59 |
| Happy Death | 95 | 60 |
| Prayer of David | 96 | 61 |
| The Voice of Conscience | 98 | 62 |
| Morning Service | 99 | 63 |
| The Lay of the Prodigal, in VII Melodies: | | |
| I. The Forewarning | 101 | 64 |
| II. The Trespass | 102 | 67 |
| III. The Awakening | 103 | 68 |
| IV. The Plaint | 104 | 69 |
| V. The Avowal | 104 | 70 |
| VI. The Resolve | 105 | 71 |
| VII. The Return | 106 | 72 |
| St. Cecilia | 107 | 73 |
| St. Rose of Lima | 108 | 74 |
| St. Rose of Lima (Child's Hymn) | 110 | 75 |
| The Guardian Angels | 112 | 76 |
| The Birth of Christ | 113 | 77 |
| May Song | 115 | 78 |

## CONTENTS.

|  | PAGE. | MUSIC NOS. |
|---|---|---|
| The Altar | 116 | 79 |
| Adoro Te | 118 | 80 |
| The Broken Promise | 119 | 81 |
| The Hereafter | 120 | 82 |
| A Dirge | 121 | 83 |
| The Resurrection | 122 | 84 |
| The Guerdon | 123 | 85 |
| Emblems of Life | 125 | 86 |
| The Worship of Nature | 126 | 87 |
| The Cherished Hope | 127 | 88 |
| Antiphon from Complin | 128 | 89 |
| Neapolitan Mariner's Hymn | 129 | 90 |
| The Happy Day | 131 | 91 |
| Twilight Musings | 132 | 92 |

# CONTENTS OF AIDS TO MEMORY.

|  | PAGE. | MUSIC NOS. |
|---|---|---|
| Acts of Faith, &c. | 1 | 51 |
| The Cardinal Virtues | 2 | |
| Ten Commandments | 3 | |
| Precepts of the Church | 4 | |
| Grace | 5 | |
| A Sacrament | 5 | |
| The Seven Sacraments | 6 | |
| The Blessed Eucharist (Canticle) | 9 | 52 |
| The Four Ends of Mass | 13 | |
| The Seven Gifts of the Holy Ghost | 14 | |
| The Twelve Fruits of the Holy Ghost | 15 | |
| The Seven Corporal Works of Mercy | 7 | |
| The Seven Spiritual Works of Mercy | 7 | |
| The Seven Deadly Sins | 8 | |
| The Eight Beatitudes | 8 | |
| Four Last Things | 19 | |
| The Seven Sorrows of the Blessed Virgin | 19 | 53 |
| Aspiration | 21 | |
| The Fourteen Stations of the Cross | 21 | 54 |

# ALPHABETICAL INDEX.

|  | PAGE | MUSIC NOS. |
|---|---|---|
| A hymn of thanksgiving | 50 | 30 |
| A hymn to St. Vincent de Paul | 62 | 36 |
| Almighty Sire! I am dust | 43 | 26 |
| Almighty Father of my soul | 106 | 72 |
| An angel bent over a cradle | 87 | 55 |
| At night the wealthy citizen | 72 | 42 |
| *By Simeon old the future's told | A19 | 53 |
| Children of St. Stephen! raise | 21 | 9 |
| Child of the morning, silvery numbers | 101 | 66 |
| Christ is risen from the dead | 122 | 84 |
| Daughter of God the Father | 94 | 59 |
| Dark Clouds are over us | 129 | 90 |
| Enough of the world and its splendors | 105 | 71 |
| Ere Peace and Freedom, hand in hand | 35 | 19 |
| Far from Eden in exile we wander | 42 | 23, 25 |
| First off'ring of America | 108 | 74 |
| Forth a stern decree hath issued | 120 | 82 |
| From thy bright throne above the sky | 30 | 15 |
| God the Holy Ghost! Life-giver! | 44 | 27 |
| God of mercy, hear thy people | 78 | 45 |
| God of glory | 14 | 6 |
| Golden days and silver nights | 115 | 78 |
| Great God, I call upon thy name | 34 | 18 |
| *Great God, whatever through Thy Church | A1 | 51 |
| Hail! Virgin of virgins! | 12 | 5 |

* A indicates the page in the "Aids to Memory."

## ALPHABETICAL INDEX.

|  | PAGE. | MUSIC NOS. |
|---|---|---|
| *Hail! most holy Sacrament................ | A9 | 52 |
| Haste fond mem'ry, thy vigor recalling...... | 41 | 22, 24 |
| Hear the word........................... | 80 | 47 |
| Help of Christians, while the combat........ | 67 | 39 |
| *Holy Spirit, in my bosom.................. | A15 | 64 |
| Holy Stephen, Chief of Martyrs............. | 5 | 1 |
| How kind it is of you to come.............. | 38 | 21 |
| I hear a voice from Bethlehem.............. | 79 | 46 |
| I bow before thee, unseen Deity............. | 118 | 80 |
| I love to see a tear-drop................... | 84 | 48 |
| In a dream I saw the seasons............... | 113 | 77 |
| In highest heaven, where stands the throne.. | 25 | 12 |
| I passed a rose at early morn............... | 125 | 86 |
| I too have stood among the band............ | 104 | 70 |
| It is the hour—it is the hour of Prayer...... | 90 | 57 |
| Jane de Chantal, worthy pupil.............. | 61 | 35 |
| Joseph thinks to part with Mary............ | 57 | 33 |
| Know ye that Angels ..................... | 112 | 76 |
| Let a pious prayer be said.................. | 121 | 83 |
| Lord! when a silvery star.................. | 46 | 28 |
| Lord of Hosts! from the home of our childhood | 40 | 23, 25 |
| Most Holy Trinity, One God................ | 75 | 44 |
| My heart is sad and heavy................. | 104 | 69 |
| Near thy servant dying.................... | 95 | 60 |
| Now is the Day-star....................... | 99 | 65 |
| O brightness of eternal light............... | 48 | 29 |
| Oftentimes when angry billows............. | 59 | 34 |
| Oh how shall we praise thee, Cecilia........ | 107 | 73 |
| O Magdalen! O Magdalen.................. | 64 | 37 |
| Oh, Mary! Mother Mary!.................. | 22 | 10 |
| Punish me not in the day of thy wrath...... | 96 |  |
| Queen of Angels .......................... | 92 | 58 |

## ALPHABETICAL INDEX. xiii

| | PAGE | MUSIC NOS. |
|---|---|---|
| Rejoice, oh ye children of bondage! | 19 | 8 |
| Salva nos Domine vigilantes | 128 | 89 |
| Skies of purple and gold | 103 | 68 |
| Slumber, haste! on dewy pinions | 26 | 13 |
| Snow and rain have vanished | 68 | 40 |
| Soul, awaken, in sadness why languish? | 42 | 22, 24 |
| Spirits that languish | 33 | 17 |
| *Spirit of Holiness | A14 | 63 |
| Star of the ocean! | 29 | 14 |
| This day is a day of rejoicing | 131 | 91 |
| The earth, O Lord, rejoices | 11 | 4 |
| The vision—the vision of Death and its terrors | 86 | 50 |
| The tear of innocence—how bright | 32 | 16 |
| *The Son of God came down from heaven | A21 | 54 |
| The Messenger Angel descending at night | 8 | 3 |
| The vows which I have spoken | 119 | 81 |
| The Hope which I have cherished | 127 | 88 |
| There's worship where the roses bloom | 126 | 87 |
| There once did live a little girl | 110 | 75 |
| There's music in the bubbling rill | 7 | 2 |
| There are seven bright spirits that stand | 74 | 43 |
| This is the day our Lord | 70 | 41 |
| Thy power, O Lord, is boundless power | 36 | 20 |
| *To worship at Jehovah's throne | A18 | |
| Twilight is a witching hour | 132 | 92 |
| Upon the sea at morning | 85 | 49 |
| Virgin daughter of Castile | 65 | 38 |
| What light is streaming from the skies | 55 | 32 |
| When the lowly grot of Bethlehem | 89 | 56 |
| When the air is | 53 | 31 |
| When our Saviour wished to prove | 24 | 11 |
| Where, Oh! where are the happy hours | 102 | 67 |
| Where the holy Altar stands | 116 | 79 |
| World of Grace! mysterious Temple! | 17 | 7 |
| Yes, I have heard that whisper | 98 | 62 |
| Zealous for the honor | 123 | 85 |

# LIST OF COMPOSERS.

1. SIGNOR DOMENICO SPERANZA, well known as a popular writer of music in Italy, and honored with the title of "Inneggiatore" to the royal house of Savoy, and afterward connected with the Academy of Music, New York City. Signor Speranza had under his charge as many as sixteen hundred children, belonging to the public Institutions of Turin, and received flattering testimonials from the Government, for the successful results of his system of musical instruction.

2. Mr. John M. Loretz, Jr., Organist and Director of the choir of St. Peter's Church, Brooklyn, New York. To prevent confusion the initials of Mr. Loretz have been placed at the head of each of his compositions.

3. Original words have been adapted to the following popular airs:

The French Hymn "Puissante Protectrice."
"Agathe," by Franz Abt.
Hymn of the Crusaders, by Verdi.
Hymn of the Hebrews, by Verdi.
Ach wenn du wärst mein eigen, by Kuchen.

The Canticle on the Blessed Eucharist, is set to an ancient Plain Chant, and the air of "The Worship of Nature," is by the music teacher of St. Stephen's Sunday-school, Mr. Pietro Paolicchi.

No. 90 is a popular Neapolitan air. Nos. 91 and 92 were written expressly for Sadlier's first edition by the distinguished Maestro Signor P. Rondinella.

# SONGS FOR CATHOLIC SCHOOLS.

## TO ST. STEPHEN.

Holy Stephen, Chief of Martyrs,
  Thee we hail with special love—
Mary chose thee for our patron
  'Mid all saints of heaven above:
Hear the voices of thy children,
  Kneeling fondly at thy shrine;
Fill our hearts with love for Jesus,
  With a fervent love like thine.

Fond Protector, we have loved thee
  For thy faith so bold and true;
'Twas that faith whose simple wisdom
  Overcame both Greek and Jew.
Teach us, like thee, on our foreheads
  To impress the sacred sign,
And to meet our faith's opponents
  With a courage like to thine.

Strong with rage, the heartless tyrants
　　Dragged thee to the City gate—
Stones were hurled in fearful volleys—
　　Martyr! they have sealed thy fate!
With the odor of the victim,
　　Earliest slain for Jesus' faith,
Rose a prayer imploring pardon
　　Pardon for the deed of death.

Stephen for his persecutors
　　Prays as Christ had prayed before;
And the Apostle of the nations
　　To the cause of truth comes o'er.
Proto-martyr, teach thy children
　　Good for evil to return;
Teach the hearts of unbelievers
　　Like the heart of Paul to burn.

Life in doing good thou spendest,
　　And when dying dost behold
Thy sweet Master clad in glory,
　　Mortal tongue hath never told.
Make us imitate thy virtues,
　　Blessed Saint—we are thine own,
And unite us all in heaven
　　Near the footstool of thy throne.

## THE MUSIC OF NATURE.

There's music in the bubbling rill
    That frolics o'er the mead,
That makes the silver daisy bloom,
    And laves the nodding reed.
There's music in the gentle breeze
    That whispers through the wood,
And softly sings, to mortal things,
    The praise of Nature's God.

There's music in the shower that falls
    Upon a sultry day,
To spread new verdure o'er the fields,
    And cheer the drooping spray.
There's music in the frisky lamb
    That loves the verdant sod,
And sporting sings, to mortal things,
    The praise of Nature's God.

There's music in the tiny throats
    That hail the rising sun,
That cheer the traveler's weary way,
    Across the woodland dun.
There's music in the busy bee
    That makes the flow'ret nod,
And humming sings, to mortal things,
    The praise of Nature's God.

There's music in the bright cascade
  That dashes from the steep,
Along the banks where rivers roll
  Their waters to the deep,
And, driven by the tempest's breath
  O'er foaming ocean's flood,
The billow sings, to mortal things,
  The praise of Nature's God.

Thus toward the skies an endless hymn
  Of earthly notes ascends,
And with the music of the spheres
  In daily concert blends.
One voice is harsh, one voice alone
  Through all the world's abode—
The sinner sings in praise of things
  Forbidden by his God.

## THE MESSENGER ANGEL.

The Messenger Angel descending at night,
Chased silence and shadow with music and light.

The shepherds of Bethlehem heard on the plain
The Messenger Angel, and this was his strain:
"May peace be to mortals and glory to Heaven—
The Promised of old to mankind has been given;
Rejoice at the splendors that herald his birth,
The Saviour, the Saviour has come upon earth.

"The fields are adorned with the verdure of May,
And winter's chill bosom with roses is gay;
The winds that made war on the face of the deep,
Have sought their dark caverns and lain down to sleep.
'Mid nature's glad triumph rise, mortals, arise,
The mystery viewing with holy surprise;
Rejoice at the glory that heralds his birth,
The Saviour, the Saviour has come upon earth.

"The wise men of nations advance from afar,
Led on by the shining of Jacob's bright star;
To Bethlehem's grotto their treasures they bring,
And kneel at the shrine of the heavenly King.

The Gentiles in darkness are slumb'ring no
  more,
But worship the God whom they knew not
  before,
And follow the light which announces his
  birth—
The Saviour, the Saviour has come upon
  earth."

Yet chanted the Seraph, when rapturous strains
From thousands of angels awakened the plains;
Ethereal splendor encircled the throng
That caught up his theme and re-echoed his
  song.
The burden was swelled by each heavenly
  voice:
"The Expected is come: happy mortals re-
  joice!
Rejoice at the glories that herald his birth—
The Saviour, the Saviour has come upon
  earth."

## MORNING PRAYER.

The earth, O Lord, rejoices,
    And sings with glad acclaim,
A hymn of many voices,
    In honor of thy name.
We join the happy chorus,
    That hails the morning light;
And bless the Lord that o'er us,
    Kept loving watch all night.

Our every thought and action,
    We offer up to thee;
From folly and distraction,
    We beg thee keep us free.
Let no profane example,
    No censure, no applause,
Lead us this day to trample,
    O Lord, upon thy laws.

It pleased thee, Lord, to make us,
    That we might serve thee here;
Let not thy grace forsake us,
    But keep us in thy fear.
Preserve our life, O Father,
    That we may serve thee still;
But let us lose it rather
    Than disobey thy will.

## HAIL! VIRGIN OF VIRGINS

Hail! Virgin of virgins!
   Thy praises we sing,
Thy throne is in heaven,
   Thy Son is its King.
The Saints and the Angels
   Thy glory proclaim;
All nations devoutly
   Bow down at thy name.

Let all sing of Mary,
   The mystical Rod,
The Mirror of Justice,
   The Handmaid of God.
Let valley and mountain
   Unite in her praise;
The sea with its waters,
   The sun with its rays.

Let souls that are holy
   Still holier be,
To sing with the angels
   Sweet Mary, of thee
Let all who are sinners
   To virtue return,
That hearts without number
   With thy love may burn.

Thy name is our power,
   Thy love is our light;
We praise thee at morning,
   At noon and at night.
We thank thee, we bless thee,
   When happy and free;
When, tempted by Satan,
   We call upon thee.

The world does not love thee,
   Oh beautiful one!
Because it despises
   The cross of thy Son.
But thou art the Mother
   Of all Adam's race;
The birth-stain of Eva
   'Tis thine to efface.

Oh! be then our Mother,
   And pray to the Lord,
That all may acknowledge
   And worship His Word;
That good men with courage
   May walk in His ways,
And bad men converted
   May join in His praise.

## THE INVOCATION.

God of glory,
   God of might,
Foe of error,
   Friend of right,—
Roll the tempest
   Far away,
Smile in sunbeams
   As we pray.

We are prostrate
   At thy throne,
Knowing, fearing
   Thee alone.
Thou art Master
   Of us all,—
Nations by Thee
   Stand or fall.

Who can conquer
   Thee, O, Lord?
What is stronger
   Than Thy word?
What Thou blessest
   Must prevail;
What Thou cursest
   Can but fail.

At thy bidding,
  Like a scroll,
Heaven its blue arch
  Did unroll.
Stars and planets
  Sprung to light,
From the bosom
  Of the night.

'Tis thy wisdom
  Guides the sun,
Till his daily
  Race is run;
And when evening
  Spreads its haze,
Silver moonbeams
  Speak Thy praise.

O'er the waters,
  At thy word,
Earth upheaving
  Owned its Lord.
Yearly traveling,
  Space immense,
Earth still blesses
  Providence.

To thine image
　Man was made,
And in Eden's
　Sunny glade,
Blest with graces
　Bright and strong,
Good to follow,
　Shunning wrong.

Led by Satan
　To rebel,
From thy favor
　Soon he fell.
But as Adam
　Stood, we stand,
Raised by Jesus'
　Outstretched hand.

God of Mercy,
　Truth and Right,
Give Thy ransomed
　Children light,
Here His sacred
　Law to prize,
And to see Him
　In the skies.

## THE CHURCH.

World of Grace! mysterious Temple!
  Holy, Apostolic, One!
Never changing, ever blessing
  Ev'ry age and ev'ry zone;
Church, sweet mother! may all nations
  Know thee, love thee as of yore,
May thy children learn to prize thee,
  Daily, hourly, more and more.

Where on earth the hapless region
  Not illumined by her light?
Where the shore her saintly heralds
  Never gladdened with their sight?
Unconfined by wave or mountain,
  Spreads her voice from pole to pole,
Threat'ning Hell or pledging Heaven
  To the pure or guilty soul.

Vainly did the haughty Roman
  Smite her cheek with power's rod,
Vainly did the subtler Attic
  Spread his toils where'er she trod.
Through the adverse crowd she wended,
  In the triumph of her might,
Baffling Warrior, Sage, and Sophist,
  Skilled in wiles or bold in fight.

From his couch of fragrant roses
  She has torn the Sybarite,
She has checked the rushing Vandal
  In the hottest of the fight;
She has tracked the Northern Savage
  Even to his rocky den;
She has tamed the vengeful Huron
  Wandering in the woody glen.


She has written in the tablets
  Of the infantine Chinese;
She has sung amid the bowers
  Of the happy Bengalese;
She has snatched the trembling Hindoo
  From the smoking funeral pile;
She has lit the dusky features
  Of the bond-slave with a smile.


All of Truth, and naught of Error,
  Is her dowry—hers alone;
While her life of inward beauty
  Knows—hopes—loves the Triune One.
From the heart of her Beloved
  Flows a fount in seven-fold stream,
Whence her children draw the waters
  Lit by Heaven's quickening beam.

Church of God! mysterious Temple!
　Holy, Apostolic, One!
Never changing, ever blessing
　Ev'ry age and ev'ry zone.
Church, sweet mother! may all nations
　Know thee, love thee as of yore,
May thy children learn to prize thee,
　Daily, hourly, more and more.

## THE ASCENSION.

Rejoice, oh ye children of bondage!
　The night of your grief has gone by,
And bright as the sun is at morning,
　Your Lord has ascended on high.
Lift up the bright portals of glory,
　Blest Angels, to let in your King,
And hasten the hymn of His triumph,
　On golden harps bravely to sing.

He bowed Him in death, as a victim,
　To atone for the crime of the world;
Sin's sceptre from Sin He hath wrested,
　Death's dart against Death He hath hurled.
Great Father, the shafts of Thy anger
　Now happily idle will be—
Thou smilest in peace on Thy creatures,
　No longer rebellious to Thee.

Oh Saints, that in glory refulgent,
  Burst forth from the tombs where you lay,
And back o'er a path yet untrodden,
  Come out with your Chief into day:
How looked He, how seemed He, the victor
  From worlds He had conquered below,
To worlds of ethereal splendor,
  Prepared as their Monarch to go?

Oh, none but your tongue, or a Seraph's,
  May tell of the Infinite One,
Whom kings in their glory resemble,
  As glow-worms resemble the sun.
Yet we can exult in your triumph,
  Ye servants and friends of the Lord—
We hope, humbly hope yet to share it,
  Through grace of the all-saving Word.

This day, in the heart of poor mortals
  Reign gladness and peace.—It is well!
This day the chill shadow of sadness
  Should darken no dwelling but Hell.
This day, let the prayers of the youthful,
  Like incense, to Heaven ascend,
And gain for the souls of the ransomed
  The grace to love God to the end.

## THE BLESSING.

CHILDREN of St. Stephen! raise
High the grateful notes of praise;
With the voice the heart should swell,
While the orison you tell:
    Nos cum prole pia,
    Benedicat Virgo Maria!

Jesus, God's Incarnate Word!
Mary, mother of our Lord!
Bless us, while our choral song,
Peals the sacred walls along:
    Nos cum prole pia,
    Benedicat Virgo Maria!

Bless our Church, the common home,
Where the faithful daily come,—
Now to breathe a thankful prayer,
Now to pour their sorrows there!
    Nos cum prole pia,
    Benedicat Virgo Maria!

Bless our priest who at the shrine,
Offers up the Host Divine,—
Or God's justice to adore,
Or His mercy to implore!
    Nos cum prole pia,
    Benedicat Virgo Maria!

Bless our parents, teach them still
All their duties to fulfill;
Still aright our steps to lead,
By their word, and by their deed.
    Nos cum prole pia,
    Benedicat Virgo Maria.

Bless us when in school we learn,
When we play, or home return,—
And when fails this mortal breath,
Hear us praying at our death.
    Nos cum prole pia,
    Benedicat Virgo Maria.

## PRAYER AGAINST TEMPTATION.

[Arranged for the French hymn "*Puissante Protectrice.*"]

Oh, Mary! Mother Mary!
  We place our trust in thee—
Our faith shall never vary,
  Though weak the flesh may be.
Too oft with steps unwary,
  From duty's path we've bent:
Oh, Mary! Mother Mary!
  Thou teach us to repent.

The grisly form of terror
  Now rises on our way;
Now more seductive error
  Would lead our feet astray.
Satan is strong and wary,
  But thou wilt crush his might:
Oh, Mary! Mother Mary!
  Strengthen us in the fight.

From dangerous occasions
  That blind, imprudent eyes—
From treacherous persuasions
  That point not to the skies—
From mirth too light and airy,
  From thought too sad and deep:
Oh, Mary! Mother Mary!
  Thy little children keep.

Let us remember ever
  The presence of the Lord;
To serve him let's endeavor,
  In thought, in deed, in word.
As Monster, or as Fairy,
  Satan may take the field—
But Mary! Mother Mary!
  Thy name will be our shield.

## HOLY COMMUNION.
### AIR—AGATHE.

When our Saviour wished to prove
All the fullness of his love,
He gave us ere life was spent
The thrice Holy Sacrament.
It is here his burning heart
Would to all its flames impart;
Thus He speaks with love divine,
Give me, oh give me that heart of thine.

When the dark and stormy night
Fills the soul with wild affright;
From the cloud wherein he hides
Soon a ray of comfort glides.
Where the tear of penance falls,
Where the voice of sorrow calls;
Still He speaks with love divine,
Give me, oh give me that heart of thine

Can the Saint's ecstatic flight—
Can the wingèd Seraph's might,
To their Lord approach more near
Than do we poor sinners here?
God Himself we here receive,
Nobler gift He cannot give;
Yet He breathes with love divine,
Give me, oh give me that heart of thine.

## THE ANNUNCIATION.

In highest heaven where stands the throne
  Of Majesty supernal,
The Archangel Gabriel came alone,
  And bowed before the Eternal.
His Lord's behests received he there,
  And toward the crystal portals
He winged his way, a herald fair
  Of peace to sinful mortals.

Each heavenly choir sang hymns of thanks
  As he to each drew nearer;
And honored all adown their ranks,
  Of God's commands the bearer.
As from the gates of pearl afar
  The princely spirit wended,
Burned every conscious sun and star
  With rays more pure and splendid.

Athwart the azure firmament
  And atmospheric ocean,
He like a dazzling meteor went
  With swift but steady motion.
He reached the earth: nor shades of night
  Nor wintry snows dare meet him,
And lilies white and roses bright,
  Burst blooming forth to greet him.

He seeketh not the gilded dome
  Where reign earth's favored minions,
But in a simple Jewish home
  He rests his snowy pinions.
A lowly maiden there beholds
  The ambassador of heaven;
To her his message he unfolds—
  To her the crown is given.

Heaven's minister is heard no more
  God's wondrous works foretelling,
For he hath flown his errand o'er,
  Back to his master's dwelling.
But God fulfills the promise now,
  His Son is made our brother,
And, Mary, Queen of Virgins, thou,
  Thou art the Saviour's Mother.


## THE SLEEP OF THE INFANT JESUS

Slumber, haste! on dewy pinions
  From thy starry throne descend,
Gently toward yon little manger,
  Let thy golden wand extend.

On his mother's bosom slowly
   Lo! the Babe reclines his head;
Sweetly o'er his wearied senses
   Balmy sleep its charm hath spread.

Hark! the angry blast of winter
   Dies along the snowy plain;
Fainter grow the rippling murmurs
   Of Judea's distant main.
Through the pine-grove Cedron calmly
   Pours its waves adown the steep;
Silence reigns o'er things created
   While their God is wrapt in sleep.

But alas! a fitful shadow
   Passes o'er his features now,
Heavenly Babe, what thoughts of sorrow
   Overcast thy comely brow?
Tell, oh! tell, thou gentle mother,
   What disturbs thine Infant's rest;
Knowest thou what sad reflection
   Lurketh in his heaving breast?

Can it be this lonely grotto
   Opening on the snowy plain;
Can it be that rugged pallet
   Gives the trembling infant pain?

No! responsive to his calling
　　Gilded domes would rise from earth;
But he chose a nameless dwelling
　　For his poor and humble birth.

'Tis the heart that slumbers never
　　Though he close his wearied eyes;
Still before his mystic vision
　　Future days of strife arise.
Now he feels disgraceful fetters
　　Round his weary limbs entwined;
Now the scenes of shame and torture
　　Pass before his watchful mind.

Yet 'tis not the gloomy dungeon,
　　Thorny scourge, or glittering spear
'Tis not, Death! thy bitter chalice
　　Makes the sleeping infant fear.
'Tis the ingratitude of mortals,
　　Darker far than tyrant's art,
Reaches with its pointed arrow
　　Even the Messiah's heart.

## HYMN TO MARY.

### CHORUS.

Star of the ocean!
Mid life's commotion,
We, with devotion,
  Follow thy light.
Keep us still wary,
Lest we may vary;
Mary! Sweet Mary!
  Guide us aright.

O spotless Queen of Virgins!
  With shining lilies crowned,
Grant, we, thy youthful daughters,
  May pure, like thee, be found.
        Star of the ocean, &c.

Thou art the Queen of Martyrs,
  Crowned when thy Jesus died;
May I, thy sorrows sharing,
  Weep with thee side by side.
        Star of the ocean, &c.

To wretched mortals ever,
  Thou gentle art and kind,
In thee support and refuge,
  Repentant sinners find.
        Star of the ocean, &c.

I know that all thy glories
　No human tongue can tell;
And still, my own sweet mother!
　I know I love thee well.
　　　　　Star of the ocean, &c.

Oh, save my soul, Blest Lady!
　In Heaven with God and thee,
That I may love and praise thee
　For all eternity.
　　　　　Star of the ocean, &c.

## A CHILD'S MAY SONG.

From thy bright throne above the sky,
　Look down on us, O Mother sweet,
And smile upon the gift which I
　Here offer kneeling at thy feet.

O Mother of my God and mine,
　I've brought some simple flowers to-day,
That they may bloom upon thy shrine
　The long, long hours that I'm away.

So their sweet breath shall rise like prayer,
　When I am far from this dear spot;
Thou'lt think of me while they are here,
　And absent, I'll forget thee not.

If I were rich in gems and gold,
  All, all to thee I'd freely give;
How could I any thing withhold
  That it might please thee to receive?

But if I had a golden mine,
  And were to lay it at thy feet;
My heart not being truly thine,
  Say, would it please thee, Mother sweet!

I know it would not, and I know
  That I can only be thine own,
By loving Him who loved thee so
  That He became thine own dear son.

My heart henceforth shall be all thine,
  And I will watch, and I will pray,
That never thought or word of mine,
  May take my heart from thee away.

Oh! give a blessing now to me,
  I'll try to be so good all day,
That I may bring fresh flowers to thee,
  To make thy holy altar gay.

## THE TEAR OF INNOCENCE.

The tear of innocence—how bright
   It gushes from the eye,
It wins the sympathy of men,
   The blessings of the sky.
Before the tender infant's tongue
   Has learned to shape a sound,
It tells with simple eloquence
   His little wants around.

It droppeth from a daughter's eye
   Upon a mother's bier,
And with the spirit-world it links
   The gentle mourner here.
At Misery's piercing voice it wells
   Up from the feeling heart,
And gives the homeless wanderer,
   What gold could ne'er impart.

When Saints, remote from mortal gaze,
   Bend low in fervent prayer;
The language of the soul to God
   Is still the unbidden tear.
It fell in Bethlehem's grot—and, borne
   By Mercy up to Heaven,
Of Justice on his throne obtained,
   That man should be forgiven.

## PURGATORY.

Spirits that languish,
   In cleansing fire,
Great is your anguish,
   As your desire!
We who could lend you
   Aid and relief,
Fail to befriend you,
   Leave you to grief.

When gentle showers
   Cool the parched beds,
Languishing flowers
   Lift up their heads.
Christ's precious merits,
   Like gentle rain,
Soothe the good spirits,
   In their great pain.

To the dim region,
   Where dear ones mourn,
Love and religion
   Bid us oft turn.
Prayer hath the power
   To give them peace,
Speeding the hour
   Of their release.

## A NIGHT PRAYER.

Great God, I call upon thy name,
    And bow before thy throne,
Amid the silent shades of night,
    Unwatched, unseen, alone.
How oft amidst the glare of day,
    When pleasure's throng was nigh,
I have forgotten that I moved
    Beneath thy watchful eye!

Mine eyes have dwelt on vanities,
    Thy children should not see;
My feet forsook the pleasant paths,
    That lead to Heaven, to Thee.
I kneel and humbly own my sin,
    With many a tear and prayer;
My soul hath dwelt 'mid earthly joys,
    And found no pleasure there.

I know, I feel, my own dear Lord!
    I ne'er can happy be,
Unless my soul shall centre all
    Its hopes, its love in thee.
Be faithful, then, my wayward heart!
    Let worldly joys grow dim;
Thou'rt made for God, and never wilt,
    Find rest unless in Him.

## SONG OF THE UNION.
### Published in 1850.

Ere Peace and Freedom, hand in hand,
Went forth to bless this happy land,
   And make it their abode,
It was the footstool of a throne;
But now no sceptre here is known,
   No King is feared but God.

Americans uprose in might,
And triumphed in th' unequal fight,
   For Union made them strong:—
Union! the magic battle-cry
That hurled the tyrant from on high,
   And crushed his hireling throng!

That word since then hath shone on high
In starry letters to the sky—
   It is our country's name!
What impious hand shall rashly dare
Down from its lofty peak to tear
   The banner of her fame?

The spirits of th' heroic dead,
Who for Columbia fought and bled,
   Would curse the dastard son,
Who should betray their noble trust,
And madly trample in the dust,
   The charter which they won.

From vast Niagara's gurgling roar
To Sacramento's golden shore,
 From east to western wave,
The blended vows of millions rise,
Their voice re-echoes to the skies—
 "The Union we must save!"

The God of nations, in whose name
The sacred laws obedience claim,
 Will bless our fond endeavor
To dwell as brethren here below—
The Union then, come weal, come woe,
 We will preserve forever!

## THE BLESSED EUCHARIST.

Thy power, O Lord, is boundless power,
 Thy love is boundless love;
And for that love and by that power
 Thou comest from above.
   Son of God! we bow before thee
   Blessed Saviour! we adore thee.

Beneath the outward forms of bread,
 That seems but is not here,
The living manna lies concealed,
 The Lamb of God is near.
   Son of God! we bow before thee,
   Blessed Saviour! we adore thee.

We cannot see thee, yet we know
  Thou'rt present, dearest Lord;
'Tis not the sight that guides our mind—
  'Tis faith in thy true word.
    Son of God! we bow before thee,
    Blessed Saviour! we adore thee.

Were all the beauty of thy face
  Unveiled to mortal sight,
We'd fall to earth; we could not bear
  The blaze of heaven's full light.
    Son of God! we bow before thee,
    Blessed Saviour! we adore thee.

Come, Lord, to me, and all my heart
  Shall ever be thine own
And I shall care and I shall sigh
  For thee—for thee alone.
    Son of God! we bow before thee,
    Blessed Saviour! we adore thee.

Thy love for me, and mine for thee,
  In one bright flame now burns,
And thus thy love for my poor soul
  To thee, sweet Lord, returns.
    Son of God! we bow before thee,
    Blessed Saviour! we adore thee.

O bread of angels, food of life,
 Be thou my life, my love,
My strength and comfort here below,
 My joy in heaven above.
  Son of God! we bow before thee,
  Blessed Saviour! we adore thee.

## CHILD'S HYMN TO THE GUARDIAN ANGEL.

How kind it is of you to come,
Bright angel, from your starry home,
And watch by night and watch by day,
Beside a sinful child of clay!
How good and pure I ought to be,
Who always live so near to thee,
Beneath thine eyes the whole day round,
Where'er I tread is holy ground.

And if I had my wish I would,
Dear angel mine! be always good,
This minute I would rather die,
Than say bad words or tell a lie.
I always feel disposed this way,
Whene'er I kneel me down to pray,
But I forget when church is o'er,
And am as naughty as before.

Oh blessed guardian, kind and mild,
Have pity on a poor weak child,
And pray that God will make me strong,
To do the right and shun the wrong.
Whenever I commit a sin,
I feel my very heart within
Grow chill and heavy like a clod,
Because I have offended God.

But I would love to fear the Lord,
And shun each sinful deed and word,
Not do the sin, then feel the force
Of bitter shame and keen remorse.
I wish to think of God and thee
Whenever pretty things I see,
Till every flower that gems the sod
Shall make me think of thee and God.

Inspired by faith, I wish to hear,
Thy gentle footfall strike my ear;
Before thy radiant face to bow,
And feel thy kiss upon my brow.
Thy broad white wings shall be my shield,
While battling on life's dusty field;
Thine arms enfold me when I die,
And waft me homeward to the sky.

## HYMN OF THE CRUSADERS.

FROM "I LOMBARDI," BY VERDI.

O Signore dal tetto natio.

Lord of Hosts! from the home of our childhood
Thou hast called us with promises holy,
We marched boldly through waste and through
  wildwood,
    Sure to conquer, yet ready to die.
But our looks are dejected and lowly,
And thy servants are bowed down with sorrow.
Shall the cross and its warriors to-morrow
    Prove a scoff when the Paynim draw nigh?
We remember dear Lombardy's mountains,
    Her vineyards, her fields rich in glory,
Her fresh breezes, her murmuring fountains,
    The green bowers that wave in her land.
Ah! fond mem'ry, thou'rt scarcely a blessing,
    Thou recallest our childhood's sweet story,
But we're roused from thy dreamy caressing,
    By the glow of the hot desert sand.

## HYMN OF THE HEBREWS.
### FROM "NABUCO," BY VERDI.

*Va pensiero sull' ali dorate*

Haste, fond mem'ry, thy vigor recalling,
Haste away to the valleys and mountains,
Where the breeze o'er Judea's bright fountains
Cools the air of our dear native land.

Hover fondly o'er Jordan's clear waters,
Mark the turrets of Sion now falling;
Oh! Judea, thy sons and thy daughters
Weep for thee on this barbarous strand.

Harp of gold! hast thou parted with glory,
That thou hangest unstrung on the willow?
Oh! as billow rolls on after billow,
Let the music rush o'er thy bright chords.

Dark and sad, like poor Solyma's story,
Breathe a dirge mixed with deep sighs of sor-
    row,
Or from mem'ry some bright ditty borrow,
Bearing courage and strength in its words.

## RECOLLECTION.
*Air—O Signore dal tetto natio.*

Far from Eden in exile we wander,
  'Mid the darkness of night and of error;
And of dreams we grow fonder and fonder,
  If we call not, O Lord, on thy power.
While we pray, every vision of terror
  Melts away like the dew-drops at morning,
And the wiles of the proud tempter scorning,
  We are free as in Eden's lost bower.

Oh this world when it scatters its flowers,
  When it gathers its trophies around me,
May beguile for a few fleeting hours,
  But the heart, Lord, is wretched, or thine.
Then before death has spread his dark pinion,
  And the spell of its shadow has bound me,
Let me bow to my Saviour's dominion,
  Let his glory or cross still be mine!

## ENCOURAGEMENT.
*Air—Va pensiero sull'ali dorate.*

Soul, awaken, in sadness why languish?
  Break away from thy fears and thy fetters,
Feel the courage that rouses and betters,
  Leave the desert its silence and gloom.

Look abroad, honest work has its beauty,
    Earnest hearts can forget their own anguish,
And can toil in the vineyard of duty,
    While the sluggard sits wailing his doom.

Saddest hearts 'neath their ashes have embers,
    That will glow if we do good to others;
For the prayers of our needier brothers,
    Turn to blessings and follow us home.

We are all of one body the members,
    Here to-day be we sharers in sorrow;
For we hope to be sharers to-morrow,
    In the light of the glory to come.

## TO THE EVER BLESSED TRINITY.

ALMIGHTY Sire! I am dust,
Unbounded power is thine;
Weakness and want are mine,
In thee my love, my trust.

CHORUS.

Sanctus Deus,
Sanctus fortis,
Sanctus immortalis,
Miserere nobis!

Eternal Son! I am blind,
The light of light is thine;
Error and doubt are mine,
Guide thou my trembling mind.
 Chorus—Sanctus Deus, etc.

Oh Holy Ghost! Give heart,
All life, all love are thine,
Frailty and grief are mine,
To me thy warmth impart.
 Chorus—Sanctus Deus, etc.

## HYMN TO THE HOLY GHOST.

God the Holy Ghost! Lifegiver!
 Of the Three Blest Persons Third,
Humbly kneeling we adore thee,
 With the Father and the Word.
Thou art of the selfsame nature,
 As the Father and the Son,
Equally from both proceeding,
 Thou dost bind them both in One.

They distinct in person only,
 Into thee breathe life divine;
And the essence of the Godhead,
 Flows into their life from thine.

In the far eternal ages,
　With the Father and the Word,
Thou didst reign in might and glory,
　Equal God and equal Lord.

Life and love have their beginning,
　And they have their end in thee;
Life cannot endure without thee,
　Love without thee cannot be.
Thou hast spoken by the Prophets
　In Judea's favored land,
While they wrote the sacred pages,
　Thou hast guided mind and hand.

Thou didst clothe the Word Eternal
　With our flesh in Mary's womb,
When he came on earth to save us
　From our sinful parents' doom.
Like a dove near Jordan's waters,
　Hov'ring o'er the promised one,
Madest known to Jew and Gentile,
　God's beloved only Son.

When the chosen Twelve lay hidden,
　From Judea's watchful ire,
They beheld and felt thee coming,
　In the form of tongues of fire.

Boldly from the upper chamber,
  By thee led they sallied forth,
Preaching Christ and working wonders,
  In all regions of the earth.

Holy Spirit, in thy beauty
  Ever ancient, ever new,
Guard the Church which thou hast founded,
  Keep her children firm and true.
Never let us sin against thee,
  Paraclete! we trust in thee!
With thy fruits and gifts surround us,
  'Till thy face in heaven we see.

## HYMN OF PRAISE.

Lord! when a silvery star
Gleams in the blue depths afar,
Thoughts come to me of thine eye
Looking on us from the sky.
Lord! when a tremulous beam
Sleeps on the shadowy stream,
Thoughts come to me of thy love,
Brightening our hearts from above.

### Chorus.

All that is winning and fair,
Speaks of thy love and thy care;
All that is noble and grand,
Speaks of the power of thy hand.
All things are made by thy word,
All thy works praise thee, O Lord;
Gladly our voices we raise,
Joining the hymn of thy praise.

If to the hills I retreat,
There I find prints of thy feet;
Down in the caves of the sea,
Coral and gems tell of thee.
Deep in the shadowy wood,
Deer for their young ones get food;
Wolves even find in their lair,
Proofs of thy pitying care.

Chorus—All that is winning, etc.

Cheered by thy dew and thy rain,
Orchard and field bloom again;
All the bright flowers are by thee,
Scattered o'er hillock and lea.
There's not a fish in the seas,
There's not a bird in the trees,

Thou dost not reach with thine eyes,
From thy bright throne in the skies.

CHORUS—All that is winning, etc,

Children of God, all your days,
Joyfully sing in his praise;
Saints and bright spirits above,
Tell of his goodness and love.
All that is noble and fair,
Tells of his power and his care;
Joyfully sing in his praise,
Children of God, all your days.

CHORUS—All that is winning, etc.

## HYMN OF TRUST.

O BRIGHTNESS of eternal light,
  I worship at thy feet;
Though all unworthy in thy sight,
  Thy mercies I repeat.
To save our souls from sin and strife,
  Is still thy work divine;
The gates of everlasting life,
  Are thine, O Lord, are thine.

I love to praise thee when the sun
   Pours forth his early light,
And when the bright stars one by one
   Come twinkling out at night.
If I am free from care and loss,
   I love to praise thy name;
If I am called to bear thy cross,
   I bless thee all the same.

If roses on my path I meet,
   I feel the gift is thine;
If briers spring to pierce my feet,
   I strive to ne'er repine.
The blessings sent to win my love,
   O Lord, I freely take;
The trials sent my faith to prove,
   I bear for thy dear sake.

Let favoring winds and friendly waves
   Speed on my little bark;
Or let me sail where ocean raves,
   And skies are chill and dark:
Let fortune smile, or let her frown,
   Let good or ill betide,
I know and feel I'm not alone,
   For thou art by my side.

Then I shall on my journey go,
  And fear not for the end;
It matters not who is my foe,
  If Jesus is my friend.
In thee, sweet Lord, I put my trust,
  O guard me while I live;
And when this dust returns to dust,
  My soul in heaven receive.

## THANKSGIVING.

A HYMN of thanksgiving
  Lift up to the Lord;
Whatever is living,
  Hath life by his word.
Though made without merit,
  By mercy alone,
Our soul is a spirit,
  Resembling his own.

### Chorus.

With souls true and tender,
  With hearts glad and free,
Great Father! we render,
  Devout thanks to thee.

We bow down before thee,
    And fervently pray,
To love and adore thee,
    Forever and aye.

The life which he gave us,
    He guards for us still;
He watches to save us,
    From error and ill.
The dew falls from heaven,
    The grain and the fruit
In season are given,
    Our strength to recruit.

CHORUS—With souls true, etc

When dangers alarm us,
    He comforts our hearts;
When demons would harm us,
    He baffles their arts.
When Doubt seeks to madden
    With thoughts of despair,
His Grace shines to gladden,
    With hopes bright and fair.

CHORUS—With souls true, etc.

Each bright smile that dwelleth,
  With us in our homes,
Of God's mercy telleth,
  Since from him it comes.
Our father and mother
  He gave, and our friends;
His love, and none other,
  All good to us sends.

CHORUS—With souls true, etc.


His are the green bowers,
  Where summer birds sing,
The beautiful flowers,
  That gladden the spring;
The murmuring fountain,
  The cool breeze of morn,
The forest-clad mountain,
  The bright field of corn.

CHORUS—With souls true, etc.


He sends Faith that traces,
  The only true way,
And thousands of graces,
  That crown us each day.

Thus God here caresses,
  His servants and friends;
And evermore blesses
  Their souls when life ends.

CHORUS—With souls true, etc.

---

## HOPE.

When the air is
  Warm and bright,
Think of God who
  Made the light.
If the tempest
  Should draw nigh,
Children, fear not,
  'Twill go by.
Children, fear not,
  'Twill go by.

When your heart is
  Full of glee,
Think of God who
  Makes you free.

If some grief is
  O'er you cast,
Children, fear not,
  'Twill not last.
Children, fear not,
  'Twill not last.

If your friends are
  Firm and true,
Think of God, who
  Gave them you.
If you're helpless
  In your home,
Children, doubt not,
  Friends will come.
Children, doubt not,
  Friends will come.

If you're blest with
  Blooming health,
Think of God, who
  Gave such wealth.
If some ailment
  Try your heart,
Children, grieve not,
  'Twill depart.
Children, grieve not,
  'Twill depart.

While your life is
  To you spared,
Think of God, who
  For you cared.
If pale Death is
  At your doors,
Children, weep not,
  Heaven is yours.
Children, weep not,
  Heaven is yours.

## COMMUNION OF CHILDREN.

What light is streaming from the skies,
Revealing heaven to mortal eyes,
What voice is singing from the spheres,
Angelic hymns to mortal ears?
O holiest mystery of love!
From his resplendent throne above,
The Saviour comes unseen to dwell,
Among the souls he loveth well.

He cometh not in fiery cloud,
He speaketh not in thunder loud;
He looseth not the storm-wind's breath,
To frighten men with fear of death.

But as he is in heaven above,
He comes in beauty and in love,
To fill with sweetest peace, and cheer
The hearts his own heart holds so dear.

Your soul must be as white as snow,
When to the mystic feast you go,
There to receive—O heavenly bliss!
Upon your lips the Saviour's kiss.
You will become his happy guest,
A flood of joy shall fill your breast;
All earthly cares shall fade away,
As night before the approach of day.

The bread of angels will impart
New vigor to your mind and heart;
You will become a child of truth,
Endowed with everlasting youth.
New virtues in you shall abound,
Like flowers of spring in goodly ground;
The Lord is with you! his right arm
Shall guard your future life from harm.

O happy soul, O happy soul,
Thy race is sure and heaven the goal;
Thy Saviour loveth thee so well,
That he is come with thee to dwell.

O thou art like an Angel now,
Cloud not with sin thy radiant brow;
Live on in hope and purity,
And God will give his heaven to thee.

## ST. JOSEPH.

#### HIS SORROWS AND JOYS.

### I.

Joseph thinks to part with Mary,
Doubt perplexes him and grieves him,
But an Angel's voice relieves him,
  And explains the mystery.

  Dear St. Joseph, I implore thee,
    By the sorrows that oppressed thee,
    By the many joys that blessed thee,
      Dear, St. Joseph, pray for me.

### II.

Seeing Christ in Bethelém's manger,
Sorrow fills his heart so tender;
He's consoled by sudden splendor,
  And celestial melody.
    Dear St. Joseph, etc.

### III.

Joseph weeps, he has to witness
Jesus in the temple bleeding;
But is cheered the future reading
  In Old Simeon's prophecy.
    Dear St. Joseph, etc.

### IV.

Now they fly from ruthless Herod,
And our Saint is filled with sadness;
Angels soon bring light and gladness,
  To the Holy Family.
    Dear St. Joseph, etc.

### V.

Jesus lost! and vainly seeking,
His fond parents droop and languish;
But they soon forget their anguish,
  In their Saviour's company.
    Dear St. Joseph, etc.

### VI.

Joseph mourns o'er man forgetful,
Of his Saviour near and present;
Yet his home is sweet and pleasant,
  Jesus shares his poverty.
    Dear St. Joseph, etc.

### VII.

Now the Patriarch is dying,
'Tis the hour for sad leave-taking;
Jesus comforts him, awaking
  Thoughts of blest Eternity.
    Dear St. Joseph, etc.

---

## ST. FRANCIS DE SALES.

OFTENTIMES when angry billows
  Surge and toss upon the main,
They are beaten down and vanquished,
  By a soft and steady rain.
So the gentle words of Francis
  Fell upon a warlike age;
So his virtues sweet and patient,
  Tempered Passion's gloomy rage.

Meekness made his soul her dwelling,
  From the days of early youth;
Yet as stands a rock-built tower,
  Firm he stood for right and truth.
For the alternate joys and sorrows
  Of the Priesthood set apart,
He combined a Martyr's courage,
  With a gentle Virgin's heart.

Why did countless unbelievers
  Round the holy Prelate crowd?
Why did sinners at his preaching
  Raise their voice and weep aloud?
'Twas the loving soul within him,
  Shining through his form and face,
Drew his yielding willing hearers
  To his fatherly embrace.


Pure in all things as an Angel,
  Fond and simple as a child,
With himself severe and watchful,
  With the poor and fallen mild;
He proclaimed that passion leads us
  O'er a dark and thorny road,
And that men are happy only
  When they love and serve their God.


Holy Francis, now in heaven,
  Sweetly guide thy children still,
To a life of true devotion,
  Free from doubt and free from ill.
Let the love of God inspire us,
  Let all earthly joys grow dim,
So that we may learn to suffer,
  Learn to live and die for him.

## ST. JANE FRANCES DE CHANTAL.

Jane de Chantal, worthy pupil
  Of the great and good De Sales,
Thee our song with pious homage,
  On this festal morning hails.
Nurtured in thy father's castle,
  When a sweet and gentle girl;
Thou wert never spoiled by grandeur,
  Nor by fashion's giddy whirl.

On the shining star of duty
  Ever dwelt thy watchful eye,
For thy hope and love were centred
  In thy home beyond the sky.
Happy was the gallant baron,
  He who claimed thee for his bride;
Thou wert of his home the treasure,
  Of his race the flower and pride.

And yet thou, O sainted Lady,
  Peace and pardon didst award,
To the friend whose careless weapon
  Put to death thy noble Lord.
Ah, the Saints of God were ever
  Truly humble, truly meek;
Let us learn from their example,
  Never for revenge to seek.

In a bright and happy household,
  Passed thy useful widowhood;
There thy children grew up round thee,
  Like their mother, pure and good.
Yet from ties so dear and tender,
  From the friends that loved thee well,
Jesus drew thee gently onward,
  To the cloister and the cell.

Called by heaven, many daughters
  Soon were gathered in thy school;
Many still, from every nation,
  Bless thy wise and loving rule.
Holy Foundress, let thy spirit
  Guide us on the upward road;
Let us, walking in thy footsteps,
  "Die to self and live to God."

## ST. VINCENT DE PAUL.

A HYMN to St. Vincent de Paul,
  The Apostle of brotherly love!
He cared for the great and the small,
  As sons of one Father above.
He taught men in Luxury's dome,
  The wisdom that feareth the Lord;
He taught men in Poverty's home,
  The patience that trusts in His word.

From parents by want driven wild,
　　From bye-ways for crime set apart,
He gathered the shivering child,
　　And cradled it next his warm heart.
From snares but too artfully laid,
　　By bold men and bad men of earth,
He rescued the innocent maid,
　　And led her to honor and worth.

The floor of the dungeon he trod,
　　Mid outcries of anguish and spite;
The smile of the servant of God,
　　O'er hearts that were hopeless shed light.
He from the dark river hard by,
　　Drew back the poor victim of shame;
He bade her look up to the sky,
　　And hope in the all-saving Name.

The Daughters of Vincent de Paul
　　Went forth on their mission of love,
They are sisters to each one and all
　　Who are dear to Our Father above.
Whenever a crime or an ill
　　Dims the image and likeness divine,
They are guided by Charity still,
　　To watch where the wretched recline.

What suffering of fallen mankind
　　Has Vincent passed by or forgot ?
Where failed he with heart and with mind
　　To better Humanity's lot ?
Then love him, and pray God to send,
　　Your life may resemble his own;
See in each man a brother, a friend,
　　Love sinners, and hate sin alone.

## ST. MARY MAGDALEN.

O MAGDALEN! O Magdalen,
　　I see thee in the Supper Hall,
I hear the sob thou gavest then,
　　I see the tear-drop gush and fall.
A sorrow something like thy own,
　　Is busy in my sinful heart;
But while I sigh and while I moan,
　　I feel I am not what thou art.

O Magdalen, O Magdalen,
　　I see thee Penitent and Blest,
And ask my guilty conscience when
　　It will consent to give me rest!
I ceased to fight 'gainst Sin and Hell,
　　I drank the World's empoisoned cup,
And found he must in misery dwell,
　　Who meanly gives the battle up.

O Magdalen, O Magdalen,
   Thy Saviour saw thy grief, thy love;
He blessed thee and forgave thee then,
   He sees me now from heaven above.
Thou standest near his throne—oh pray,
   Dear Saint! and let thy prayer be such,
That I, unworthy sinner, may,
   Be pardoned too by loving much.

## ST. TERESA.

Virgin daughter of Castile,
   All thy country's olden worth,
All her knightly fire and zeal,
   Burned within thee from thy birth.
Ah, the world with cunning art,
   Strove its idols to enthrone,
In the warm and noble heart,
   God had formed to be his own.

Thou wert led from love so vain,
   Thou wert scourged with sorrow's rod,
And thy body drooped with pain,
   But thy soul rose nearer God.
He consoles thy spirit now,
   With a sense of joyful rest;
Heavenly wisdom bathes thy brow,
   Heavenly rapture fills thy breast.

Now a dryness and a gloom
　O'er thee pass and try thy love,
Soon they vanish—light hath come,
　Dew hath fallen from above.
Let the world annoy thee sore,
　And with thorns thy pathway sow,
Jesus braved its scorn before,
　Wore its thorns upon his brow.

Far away from worldly strife,
　And forgetting human care,
Thou didst live a higher life,
　Nourished by the food of prayer.
See! the Angel hovers near,
　With his mystic fiery dart,
Heavenly music fills thine ear,
　Heavenly love has pierced thy heart.

Neither earth nor heaven to thee
　Could a dearer joy afford,
Than in mind and heart to be
　Still united with thy Lord.
Teach thy children how we may
　Know him, love him, serve him here,
And behold his face one day,
　In a better, higher sphere.

## MARY, HELP OF CHRISTIANS.

Help of Christians, while the combat
Deepens round us, we beseech thee,
Let our prayerful voices reach thee,
  Grant us succor lest we fall.
Life on earth is ceaseless warfare,
Many fears and cares oppress us,
Many bitter foes distress us,
  Thou wilt save us from them all.

First the artful world allures us,
All its wealth before us flaunting,
Of its ease and freedom vaunting,
  Of its pomps and vanity.
Woe to us if we are dazzled,
By its boldness and profusion,
Time dispels the world's illusion,
  Death unveils its treachery.

Next the Devil would ensnare us,
Of a godlike wisdom telling,
Man might conquer by rebelling,
  'Gainst the laws of Truth and Right.
Woe if Doubt and Pride should lead us,
Into Satan's fatal error,
Life would be a day of terror,
  Death a mute and starless night.

Last the Flesh gives baneful counsel,
Whispering of a life of pleasure,
Without end and without measure,
   Where its languid votaries dwell.
Woe if we by sense are blinded,
Life in idle pastime spending
We should barter bliss unending,
   For vain joys that lead to hell.


Help of Christians, while the combat
Deepens round us, we beseech thee
Let our prayerful voices reach thee,
   Grant us succor lest we fall.
Life on earth is ceaseless warfare,
Many fears and cares oppress us,
Many bitter foes distress us,
   Thou wilt save us from them all.

## THE MONTH OF MARY.

Snow and rain have vanished,
   Winds have ceased to wail,
Gloomy winter's banished
From the hill and dale.

CHORUS.

Gentle Mother hear us,
　At thy altar pray,
Queen of Saints, be near us
　On this sweet May-day.

Spring hath come with flowers,
　Spring hath come with light,
Soft and rosy hours
　Fill the day and night.

 CHORUS—Gentle Mother, etc.

Stars above us gleaming,
　Tell of Mary's worth,
Blossoms 'round us teeming,
　Speak her praise to earth.

 CHORUS—Gentle Mother, etc.

Here below deserving
　She was found alone,
God from sin preserving,
　Chose her for his own.

 CHORUS—Gentle Mother, etc.

Grace as to none other,
  Grace to her was given,
She became the mother,
  Of the King of heaven.

  Chorus—Gentle Mother, etc.

God bestowed upon her
  Glories all her own,
Earth's sublimest honor,
  Heaven's queenly throne.

  Chorus—Gentle Mother, etc.

Taught by Him we love her,
  In our simple way,
Placing none above her,
  On this sweet May-day.

  Chorus—Gentle Mother, etc.

## THE LORD'S DAY.

### Chorus.

This is the day our Lord
  Hath chosen for his own;
Come, mortals, from your toil,
  And worship at his throne.

Lift up your hearts in prayer,
　　And let your wants be known;
This is the day our Lord,
　　Hath chosen for his own.


The Lord made heaven and earth,
　　The stars, the moon, the sun,
And on the seventh day,
　　His wondrous work was done.
In six days all were made,
　　The seventh day he blessed,
Because his work was o'er,
　　And this the day of rest,

　　Chorus—This is the day, etc.


From Sinai's burning mount
　　The Lord's commands were given,
And Israel shook with fear,
　　To hear the voice of heaven.
"The Sabbath-day is mine,"
　　That voice was heard to say,
"Let all the people know,
　　And keep the Sabbath-day."

　　Chorus—This is the day, etc.

When Jesus came himself
  Our erring souls to seek,
He made the Sabbath-day
  The first day of the week;
That day the Saviour blessed,
  His glorious work was done,
And heaven's eternal rest,
  That day became our own.

    CHORUS—This is the day, etc.

## THE CHILD JESUS.

At night the wealthy citizen
  Had turned him from the door,
The only friends around him were
  The lowly and the poor.
Yet to his Father's will resigned,
  The new-born infant smiled:
This came to pass in Bethlehem,
  When Jesus was a child.

He came to do his Father's work,
  His Father's law to teach;
The Jewish doctors wondered at
  The wisdom of his speech.

In giving reasons for his faith,
   The hours away he whiled:
This came to pass in Solyma,
   When Jesus was a child.

Beneath Saint Joseph's humble roof,
   He with his mother dwelt;
His gentle words revealed to them,
   The love his bosom felt.
In every action he was kind,
   In manner always mild:
This came to pass in Nazareth,
   When Jesus was a child.

Have I been patient, wise, and good,
   When home and when abroad?
Ah no! too often I behaved
   Unlike a child of God.
In future, with my Father's will,
   I shall be reconciled,
And try to do as Jesus did,
   When Jesus was a child.

## THE SEVEN ARCHANGELS.

THERE are seven bright spirits that stand
  Near the throne of Jehovah in heaven,
And to these seven spirits, command,
  Over all the good angels, is given.
They keep watch 'neath a banner of light,
  Upon God's holy mountain unrolled;
They are clad in full armor, so bright
  That it flashes like jewels and gold.

And their faces are gentle and fair,
  And their look and their bearing sublime,
As when Lucifer fled through the air,
  From their swords, in the far-away time.
During battle they pour on the field,
  The red vials of long-treasured wrath,
And the sword of bright flame which they wield,
  Smiteth conquering Pride on his path.

But these beautiful spirits draw near
  When the clouds of adversity frown;
And the soul of the martyr they cheer,
  For they bring him the palm and the crown.
And the traveler on life's weary way,
  Finds a shield in their heavenly might,
'From the arrow that flieth by day,
  And the fiend that goes prowling by night.

As the sweet-smelling vapor ascends,
   From their censers before the Most High,
With the prayer of the just man it blends,
   And the sinful one's penitent sigh.
At our altars they worship unseen,
   Giving praise to their Lord through the night;
And the soul of the Christian they screen,
   When he fights at his death the last fight.

Great Saint Michael is chief in command
   O'er the hosts of the children of light,
Blessed Gabriel and Raphael stand
   Next in dignity, honor, and might.
All ye blessed Archangels, give ear
   To my earnest and suppliant prayer,
Let me live in the Lord's holy fear,
   And for judgment in season prepare.

## MASS HYMN.

### PART I.

*Worship.*

Most Holy Trinity, One God
   Supreme in majesty,
All power in heaven and earth is thine,
   All things belong to thee.

I offer up the Holy Mass,
  This morning, with the aim
Of blessing thy Almighty power,
  And worshipping thy name.

CHORUS.

By thy own Incarnate Word,
We adore thee, Blessed Lord.

PART II.

*Thanksgiving.*

Almighty and Eternal God,
  Thou art the good supreme;
Thou dost create us and preserve,
  Thou dost our souls redeem.
For these and all thy benefits,
  Thy mercy we adore,
And offer up the Holy Mass,
  To thank thee more and more.

CHORUS.

By thy own Incarnate Word,
We give thanks to thee, O Lord.

### PART III.
*Atonement.*

The merits of the Lamb of God,
 Can grace for all obtain;
His precious blood from every soul,
 Can wash out every stain.
I offer up his precious blood,
 To thee, my God, this day;
Oh! pardon us, and give us grace,
 No more to go astray.

CHORUS.
 Through thy own Incarnate Word,
 Grant us mercy, Blessed Lord.

### PART IV.
*Petition.*

All men have need of thee, my God,
 The just that love thy name,
The souls that sleep in sin, and those
 That feel the cleansing flame.
O grant thy blessing and thy grace,
 To all for whom we pray;
For this, O Lord, we offer up,
 The Holy Mass to-day.

CHORUS.
 Through thy own Incarnate Word,
 Hear our prayer, O Blessed Lord.

## GOD SAVE THE COMMONWEALTH.

God of mercy, hear thy people,
   While they humbly pray before thee,
   By thy goodness, we implore thee,
Save, O Lord, the Commonwealth.

Bless the land with peace and plenty,
   Keep in brotherly communion
   All the States of all the Union,
Save, O Lord, the Commonwealth.

Teach us how to love our Country,
   All her righteous laws revering,
   Hating no one, no one fearing,
Save, O Lord, the Commonwealth.

Grant America thy blessing,
   Let her children in each region
   Cherish truth and love religion;
Save, O Lord, the Commonwealth.

On the land and on the ocean,
   Bless and guard our country's banner,
   Let it ever float with honor,
Save, O Lord, the Commonwealth.

Bless the Army and the Navy,
  Guard our commerce from disaster,
  Be our Father and our Master,
Save, O Lord, the Commonwealth.

## THE HOLY INNOCENTS.

I hear a voice from Bethlehem,
  The moan of winds resembling,
It swelleth upward fitfully,
  Then falleth weakly trembling.
'Tis Rachel mourning bitterly,
  Her young in cold death sleeping,
O'er Rama spreadeth drearily,
  The chorus of her weeping.

At eve the happy shepherdess
  Home from the pasture wended,
Upon the green slept peacefully,
  The little flock she tended.
Her faithful spouse, at eventide,
  Came gladly forth to meet her,
And bright as Rose of Jericho,
  Their infant smiled to greet her.

The midnight tramp of soldiery
  Wakes Bethlem's peaceful daughters,
A cruel tyrant's jealousy
  Dyes red old Jordan's waters.
Beneath the starlight wandering,
  Meanwhile the world's Redeemer,
Avoids the prowling satellite,
  And foils the royal schemer.

Oh, mothers of fair Bethlehem,
  God wills ye weep no longer,
The new-born king of Nazareth,
  Than all your foes is stronger.
He will return to Solyma,
  And smite the tyrant gory;
He to each martyred Innocent
  Will give a crown of glory.

## DEW-DROPS OF WISDOM.

Hear the word
Of the Lord,
While in youth
Learn the truth.
Youth is bold,
Ere yet cold,
Let the earth
Know its worth.

Let its sighs
Heavenward rise,
Be its love
Fixed above.
Always fight
For the right,
And be strong
'Gainst the wrong.

Be a child
Kind and mild,
Never rude,
Ever good.
Be not bold
With the old,
Do what's fair,
Everywhere.

Never swerve
Time to serve;
Never lie,
Rather die.
Well begun
Means half done,
Do your best,
Then seek rest.

If you make
A mistake,
Do not grieve,
But retrieve.
Should you fail,
Do not wail;
That were vain,
Try again.

Kneel and pray
Every day,
In God's sight,
Morn and night.
Bravely own
To wrong done;
Then you'll do
Good anew.

Try God's will
To fulfill,
By it stand
Heart and hand.
If you err,
Don't despair,
But correct
Your defect.

Help the poor,
And be sure
Of reward,
From the Lord.
Do not shirk
Honest work;
Earning food
Makes it good.

Never walk,
Play, or talk,
With a lad
Bold and bad.
Fear the Lord,
Love his word,
Keep his ways
All your days.

Every hour
Hath the power,
To annoy,
Or give joy.
Every day
Hath its say;
Days to come
All are dumb.

Do not fret
For them yet,
Learn best how
To live now.
If in haste
Time you'll waste,
So proceed
Slow with speed.

## THE LANGUAGE OF FEELING.

I love to see a tear-drop
  Stand trembling in the eye,
Not when rude sorrow's question
  Hath wrung the heart's reply;
But when some gentle pity
  Hath softly called it up,
It sparkles like a dew-drop
  Within a violet's cup.

I love to see the sunlight
  That gilds a mantling blush,
Not when detected baseness
  Hath caused the cheek to flush;
But when true modest instincts
  Sweep heart-strings in their reach,
It shines with artless beauty,
  Like glow on downy peach.

I love to see the grandeur
   That gathers with a frown,
Not when a selfish feeling
   Hath drawn its terrors down;
But flashing forth unbidden
   Against the proud and mean,
It brightens wrath as lightning
   Illumes a stormy scene.

I love to hear the music
   That gushes with a sigh,
Not when grief drives the wretched
   To wish that they might die;
But when we turn from pleasures
   This lower world hath given,
'Tis like a pinion's flutter
   That wafts the soul to heaven.

## THE VOYAGE OF LIFE.

Upon the sea at morning,
The breeze and billow scorning,
   Youth gayly speeds away;
The birds are sweetly singing,
The early flowers are springing;
   It is the dawn of day.

The storm is darkly brewing,
And man his course pursuing,
  Must struggle or must die.
He perishes who prays not,
But he in grief delays not,
  Who seeks for aid on high.

The bark has long been sailing,
The light of day is failing,
  And age is near its doom.
But in the child of duty,
A smile of hope and beauty
  Sheds sunlight o'er the tomb.

Our bark the port is nearing,
Dear Angel Guardian steering,
  Oh, guide it on its road.
We love thee and obey thee,
Lead on, lead on, we pray thee,
  To heaven and to God.

## DEATH.

The vision, the vision of Death and its terrors,
Has made me look over my life and its errors;
  I think and I tremble to think of my sins.
The battle of life is more fierce as it closes,
He loses for earth and for heaven who loses,
  And he wins forever and ever who wins.

O, Angels and Saints, ye have passed the dim
    portal,
That leads human spirits to mansions immortal,
  Be near when the last day of earth is at hand.
Remind us to turn from the world that would
    please us,
And hope in the name and the merits of Jesus,
  Your combat is over, and with Him ye stand.

Ah! He is my Father, and He is my Master;
My soul He will rescue from gloom and disaster.
    He told me to watch, and he taught me to
        pray;
He made me to live and to love him forever.
Shall I cease to hope in him? Never, oh,
    never!
    I'll trust in his goodness till life ebbs away.

## THE ANGEL AND THE CHILD.*

An Angel bent over a cradle,
  And seemed to behold mirrored there
The light of his beautiful features,
  As though in a brook, still and fair.

---

* From the French of Reboul.

"Sweet Infant," thus gently he murmured,
   "Thou'rt like me—oh, come thou with me!
Away! we'll be happy together;
   This earth is not worthy of thee.

"The pleasures of earth are not lasting,
   They seek to enchant, but in vain,
For often bright smiles and gay laughter
   Are veils to hide passion and pain.
On days set apart for rejoicing,
   The soul may be weary and worn,
The sun, though it sets in its glory,
   Is shrouded with storm-clouds at morn.

"Shall traces of anguish and hatred
   Profane thy young brow still so clear?
Those blue eyes, so loving and tender—
   Are they to be dimmed by a tear?
Oh, no! let us fly hence together—
   Thy course shall be upward with mine;
For God, in his mercy, has spared thee
   The days that were yet to be thine.

"No mourners shall darken thy dwelling—
   No requiem lull thee to rest;
For those who are sinless as thou art,
   The last day of earth is the best."

The Angel thus ended his ditty;
  But now his bright wings he has spread,
He soars! he has gone back to heaven—
  Poor mother! thy infant is dead!

## THE VIRTUES AT BETHLEHEM.

When the lowly grot of Bethlehem
  First received the holy child,
On the shepherds' humble offering
  The Redeemer kindly smiled;
Faith, and Hope, and gentle Charity—
  Those three sisters pure and fair—
Were then led by light from heaven,
  To approach and worship there.

"Hail! thou oracle of prophets,"
  Faith advancing, said, "All hail!"
From these eyes, once dim and blinded,
  Thou hast now removed the veil."
Hope then said, "At length I see thee
  Whom th' eternal hills desired,
And my sigh hast changed to gladness,
  Thou for whom my soul aspired."

But when Charity there kneeling,
  With her downcast eyes and meek,
The devotion of her spirit
  In low tones essayed to speak,
Her sweet voice was lost in murmurs,
  And for words she vainly strove,
So she kissed the sacred forehead,
  Weeping tears of joy and love.

## THE HOUR OF PRAYER.

### PRELUDE.

(*Some voices.*)

IT is the hour, it is the hour of Prayer,
Forget the earth, forget all earthly care;
Before the Lord of Heaven and Earth bow down
With simple hearts, and worship at his throne.

### ADORATION.

(*All—pianissimo.*)

Father Almighty,
  We are but dust;
In thy great mercy
  We put our trust.

Thou art our Maker—
Thou art our Lord;
By men and angels
Thou art adored.

PRELUDE.

SUPPLICATION.

(*All—a little louder.*)

God of our fathers,
  Stretch forth thine arm;
Thou, who didst make us,
  Shield us from harm.
Teach us to name thee
  With sacred awe—
Teach us to love thee,
  And keep thy law.

PRELUDE.

PRAISE.

(*All—loud, and with joy.*)

Hear us, O Father,
  Father of all,
While with devotion
  On thee we call.

Look on thy children—
Guard us always;
Render us worthy
To sing thy praise.

## QUEEN OF ANGELS.

###### CHILD'S HYMN.

Queen of Angels,
  Pray for me,
For my heart is
  Full of thee.
Thou art nearest
  God on high—
First and fairest
  In the sky.

Blessed Mary,
  Thy sweet name
Warms my bosom
  Like a flame.
Thy dear image
  When I kiss,
All my soul is
  Rapt in bliss.

Dost thou hear us
 When we pray—
When we bless thee
 Every day?.
Yes! our Saviour
 Loves thee so,
He will surely
 Let thee know.

When we offer
 Flowers to thee,
He will surely
 Let thee see.
Thou his Mother,
 He thy Son,
What thou wishest
 Must be done.

Thou can'st never
 Try in vain
Grace or favor
 To obtain.
Thy dear Jesus
 Cannot choose
His sweet Mother
 To refuse.

Blessed Virgin,
Pray for me,
Sailing on this
Stormy sea;
Lead me onward
Through the strife—
Guide me safe to
Endless life.

## SALUTATION TO MARY.

DAUGHTER of God the Father,
O Virgin pure and mild,
I venerate and love thee—
Accept me for thy child.
My soul, and all its powers,
I consecrate to thee—
Be pleased, most holy Mother,
From sin to keep me free.

CHORUS.

Be pleased, most holy Mother,
To pray our Lord for me.

Mother of our Redeemer,
O Virgin pure and mild,
I venerate and love thee—
Accept me for thy child.

My body and its senses
  I consecrate to thee—
Be pleased, most holy Mother,
  From sin to keep me free.

CHORUS.
Be pleased, most holy Mother,
  To pray our Lord for me.

Spouse of the Holy Spirit,
  O Virgin, pure and mild,
I venerate and love thee—
  Accept me for thy child.
My heart and its affections
  I consecrate to thee—
Be pleased, most holy Mother,
  From sin to keep me free.

CHORUS.
Be pleased, most holy Mother,
  To pray our Lord for me.

## HAPPY DEATH.

NEAR thy servant dying,
  Let thy Angel stand;
On thy grace relying,
  Let my heart expand.

When these eyes no longer
  See the light of earth,
Let my faith grow stronger—
  Shine with brighter worth.

Round thy servant dying,
  Let thy Saints draw near;
On thy grace relying,
  Let me cease to fear.
When all hope shall perish
  In the help of men,
Firmer hope I'll cherish
  In thy power then.

On thy servant dying
  Let thy Mother smile;
On thy grace relying,
  I shall rest meanwhile.
When the light of Heaven
  Shineth from above,
All my sins forgiven,
  Let me die with love.

## PRAYER OF DAVID.

PUNISH me not in the day of thy wrath—
Strike me not suddenly down in my path;

Let not the enemy laugh at my fall—
Pity me, Lord, who hast pity for all.
Judge of the fatherless, hope of the weak,
Refuge and help of the lowly and meek,
Look on my wretchedness, list to my grief,
Turn for thy mercy's sake, grant me relief.


Blessed the man who hath trust in the Lord,
He shall not fall by his enemy's sword;
He in his labors shall prosper and speed—
He shall prevail in the day of his need.
God giveth ear to the upright of heart—
God from his servants will never depart;
Hope from the morning watch even till night,
Hope in his mercy, and trust in his might.


Merciful Lord, thou hast heard me before—
Show forth thy goodness and glory once more;
Waters of sorrow have gathered 'round me—
Save me, O Father, my trust is in thee.
Thou wilt give ear to my suppliant prayer—
Thou wilt deliver my feet from the snare;
They that would wrong me shall hide in their
    shame,
While I give glory and praise to thy name.

## THE VOICE OF CONSCIENCE.

Yes! I have heard that whisper,
　That small still voice within;
It said: Take care, it said: Beware—
　Do not commit a sin.
I heeded not its warning,
　I wavered, and I fell,
And felt the force of stern Remorse
　That cowed me with its spell.
Thus fare I when I go to sin,
Nor heed the warning voice within.

Yes! I have heard that whisper,
　That small still voice within;
It said: Withdraw, break not the law—
　Thou art committing sin!
I heeded not its warning,
　But stubbornly kept on,
Till grace had fled, and faith was dead,
　And peace of mind was gone.
Thus fare I when I'm doing sin,
Nor heed the accusing voice within.

Yes! I have heard that whisper,
　That small still voice within;
It said: Thou'st warred against the Lord—
　Thou hast committed sin.

I heeded not its warning,
  But walked my cheerless path,
In dread that God might seize the rod,
  And smite me in his wrath.
Thus fare I when I've done a sin,
Nor heed the chiding voice within.

In future, when that whisper,
  That small still voice within
Puts wrong and right before my sight,
  And bids me not to sin,
I'll hearken to its warning
  In every thought and deed,
Nor sin at all, or if I fall,
  I will repent with speed.
Thus I shall keep me free from sin,
And heed the friendly voice within.

## MORNING SERVICE.

Now is the Day-star
  Goldenly burning,
  Morning returning
    Calls us to prayer.
Let us not tarry,
  Let us not falter,

But to the altar
Gladly repair.

God's people 'round us,
Filled with emotion
Show their devotion,
　Bowing the head ;
Kneeling and asking,
With meek behavior,
Of the dear Saviour
　Their daily bread.

Self and its yearnings
Let us now banish,
Let the world vanish
　Out of our sight !
Then let us sweetly
Warm with the feeling
That we are kneeling
　In heaven's light.

Humble in spirit,
　Grace we are seeking,
　God to us speaking
　　Calms every fear.
Sins are forgiven,
　Doubt is a stranger,

Far is all danger,
Heaven is near.

There on the altar
Whither we're bidden,
Present though hidden
Jesus is there!
Lord! in thy temple
Prostrate before thee,
List, we implore thee
List to our prayer!

## THE LAY OF THE PRODIGAL.
### IN SEVEN MELODIES.

### I.
#### THE FOREWARNING.

Child of the morning, silvery numbers
  Temptingly urge thee on to thy fall,
Scorn the light voices haunting thy slumbers
  Child of the morning, heed not their call!
Bright flowers lure thee daintily spreading
  Over the margin of the abyss,
Woe to the heedless wanderer treading
  Thoughtlessly onward, treading amiss.

Under the wave that smiles to deceive him,
  No coral bowers flash to the light,

No golden mansions rise to receive him,
    No fairy banquet gladdens the sight.
Sad recollections, phantoms unsightly,
    Follow the hapless sinner by day,
Gloomy forebodings frown on him nightly,
    Banishing peaceful slumber away.

## II.

### THE TRESPASS.

Where, oh where, are the happy hours
    I knew ere yet by Sin defiled,
Where, oh where, are the birds and flowers
    That gave me pleasure when a child!
Dreams of vanity charmed my vision,
    And soon my peaceful home I spurned,
Then, ah, bitterly in derision
    Joy fled from me where'er I turned.

When, oh when, shall remorse and terror
    Release at length my trembling soul,
When, oh when, shall the mists of error
    Across my pathway cease to roll!
Youthful Innocence thou hast vanished,
    And to me now in wild unrest,
From the universe joy seems banished,
    For winter reigns within my breast.

## III.

#### THE AWAKENING.

Skies of purple and gold,
    Paths of velvet and down,
Wreaths of myrtle and rose,
    But no thorn in the crown.
Comrades gentle and true,
    Banquets splendid and rare,
Days all happy and bright,
    Nights all guarded from care:
This is the tale Hope told
When life was young, not old.

Skies of vapor and storm,
    Paths with briars o'ergrown,
Wreaths of cypress and yew,
    But no flower in the crown.
Friends deceitful and vile,
    Feasts of poisonous fare,
Days all bitter and blank,
    Nights all haunted with care:
This is the dirge Time sung
When life was old, not young.

## IV.

### THE PLAINT.

My heart is sad and heavy,
   The long and lonely hours
Departing pluck no thorn away,
   Returning bring no flowers.
The clouds are frowning 'round me,
   The light is fainter growing,
And friendship's voice, I hear it now,
   Not caring or not knowing.

I turn away impatient
   Where happy faces meet me,
I feel the blinding tears arise
   When laughing children greet me.
I am a prey to shadows,
   And sickly terrors wholly;
I turned from virtue to become
   The slave of Melancholy.

## V.

### THE AVOWAL.

I too have stood among the band
   Who fear dishonor more than Death;
I too the hill of Fame have scanned,
   And worn the shining laurel wreath;

But hear ye all who only live,
  Or seem to live, while men applaud—
Not all the honors earth can give
  Are worth a moment passed with God.

I too, a guest of Pleasure long,
  Have whiled away the golden hours,
Or sauntered with her idle throng
  Through marble halls and moonlit bowers;
But hear ye all who love the rose,
  And hate the thorns upon its tree—
Not all the pleasures Earth bestows
  Are worth one deed of charity.

## VI.

### THE RESOLVE.

Enough of the World and its splendors—
  I have toiled in its service too long—
Enough of unblushing offenders,
  I will break from the profligate throng.
I once had the soul of an Angel;
  I was freer and happier then;
I vow on the Holy Evangel
  To be free, to be happy again

Enough of all dreamy successes,
  For they lure with unending suspense;

Enough of all midnight excesses,
  For they immolate reason to sense.
I once had the soul of an Angel;
  I was freer and happier then;
I vow on the Holy Evangel
  To be free, to be happy again.

## VII.

### THE RETURN.

Almighty Father of my soul!
  In sorrow and in shame,
I kneel to thee, but scarcely dare
  Invoke thy holy name.
I am not worthy to be called,
  O Lord, a child of thine;
For thou art purity itself,
  And naught but sin is mine.

And yet, oh whither shall I go
  If I from thee depart?
I'll call on thee—thou'lt not despise
  A sad and lowly heart.
Thy blessed Son prayed for my soul—
  It was his dying prayer;
Forgive me, Father, for his sake,
  And save me from despair.

## ST. CECILIA.

Oh how shall we praise thee, Cecilia,
  How number what glories are thine?
To crown thee twin emblems of victory
  The palm and the lily combine.
O lady all queenly and beautiful
  Our souls are in love with thy worth,
Look down from thy glory in Paradise
  And smile on thy children of earth.

Men knew how to love God in unity,
  To praise him in words they might dare,
But thou with a full gush of melody
  Didst pour out thy spirit in prayer.
Men learned from the fire of thy charity,
  To glow and to thrill with His love;
To sing half in awe, half in ecstasy,
  As sing the bright Angels above.

O peerless, O sweetest Cecilia,
  Pure fondness for fervor and song;
Compel us to crown thee our favorite,
  'Mid all heaven's virginal throng.
A flame, O angelic enthusiast,
  Flashed up from thy heart to thy brow;
A pledge of the bliss of eternity,
  That burns in thee, beams through thee now.

Inspire us with love for the beautiful
   And so let us practise thine art;
That ever the voice of the melody,
   May chime with the voice of the heart.
One glimpse of thy radiant countenance,
   One strain of empyrean song
Would make us true lovers of purity,
   And wean us forever from wrong.

Yet, while bowing down, Queen of Harmony,
   While kissing thy robe's snowy hem
Thy children ask not that a miracle,
   Be granted to thee or to them.
Obtain for us, holy Cecilia,
   A faith and a fervor divine,
That when we have ended our pilgrimage,
   Our voices may mingle with thine.

## ST. ROSE OF LIMA.

First off'ring of America,
   On holy mother's shrine,
A hidden home, a name unknown,
   Are now no longer thine.
The light of faith from pole to pole,
   From sea to sea hath spread,
And all who love it learn to love
   The peerless Liman maid.

CHORUS.
List to our antiphon,
  Grant its request,
Pray for thy native land,
  Pray for its rest.
Pray it may ever be
  Happy and blest—
Rose of America
  Pride of the West!

A soft and radiant comeliness
  Thy virgin brow adorns,
But round the flower of innocence
  Thou plantest jealous thorns.
Thou livest for eternity,
  Thou lovest God alone,
Each day of thy young life beholds
  Some battle fought and won.
      CHORUS.

Through light of joy and shade of grief,
  Through good report and ill
Thy soul was white, and coming death
  Shall find thee faithful still.
The choir of Virgins beckon thee,
  Thy Saviour bids thee come,
Ascend, child of America,
  To thy eternal home.
      CHORUS.

O Rose of Lima's sunny land,
  O jewel of Peru,
On this new Continent of thine
  The works of grace renew.
And may we through thy prayers behold
  United in our clime,
The earnest life of this young age,
  The Faith of olden time.
    CHORUS.

## ST. ROSE OF LIMA.
### CHILD'S HYMN.

THERE once did live a little girl,
  At Lima in Peru,
The fairest little girl was she
  Her neighbors ever knew.
"Oh, see her rosy cheek," they said,
  "How prettily it glows!"
And though her name was Isabel
  They always called her 'Rose.'

But while they all admired her so
  She was not vain or proud,
But used to veil her lovely face
  And hide it from the crowd.
She feared the praises of the world
  And lived for God on high;

And though her body was on earth
  Her thoughts were in the sky.

Her family were rich and great,
  But she lived like the poor,
And ate her bread with simple herbs
  She gathered on the moor.
And when her people lost their wealth
  By fortune's giddy whirl,
She, though a lady bred and born,
  Became a servant girl.

Her crown it was a crown of thorns,
  Her life a life of pain,
But sick or well, in weal or woe,
  She never would complain.
"Increase my sufferings, O Lord,"
  Thus she would often say,
"Provided only you increase
  My love for you each day."

Our Lord in mercy smiled on her,
  And heard her pious vows,
And in a lovely vision once
  Called her his chosen Spouse.
Her trials sore are passed and o'er
  She has no earthly care,
For now Saint Rose she is in heaven,
  And praying for us there.

## THE GUARDIAN ANGELS.

Know ye that Angels
  Silently glide,
From their blest mansion,
  Down to your side.
Know ye their bright eyes,
  Watch night and day,
Lest evil spirits
  Make you their prey.

CHORUS.
Beautiful Angels,
  Keep watch and ward
Over all children
  Dear to the Lord.
By your sweet presence,
  Render us still
Steadfast in goodness,
  Proof against ill.

Blessings precede them
  While they advance,
Satan in terror
  Lowers his lance.
All the dark legions
  Flee in dismay,

Melting like morning
 Vapors away.
CHORUS—Beautiful Angels, etc.

Often their gentle
 Voice from above,
Touches our heart-strings,
 Teaches us love.
Leads us to worship
 Happily here,
Even as Angels
 In their bright sphere.
CHORUS—Beautiful Angels, etc.

## THE BIRTH OF CHRIST.*

In a dream I saw the seasons
 Coming from the stars above,
And before the new-born Saviour,
 Paying vows of Faith and Love.
Spring arrayed in roseate mantle,
 Like her flowers fresh and sweet,
Laid her amaranths and lilies,
 At the heavenly Infant's feet.

---

\* From the Italian of Rosani.

Clad in shining yellow raiment,
    Laughing Summer coming now,
Plucked, and gave a golden handful
    Of the grain that wreathed her brow.
Autumn next in motley vesture,
    Entered bearing on her head,
Filled with fruit, a little basket,
    'Twas the offering she made.

Winter stood upon the threshold,
    As if fearful that his face,
With its grim and withered features,
    Might profane that happy place.
But the Infant's glances wandered
    From the flowers, fruit, and grain,
As if seeking to discover
    Some more pleasing gift in vain.

Winter then into the sunlight
    Which the holy place adorns,
Forward steps, from 'neath his mantle,
    Drawing forth a crown of thorns.
To that thorny wreath the Infant
    Stretches forth his hands in play,
While his gentle mother, shuddering,
    Turns her troubled eyes away.

But Love, heavenly Love, was able
    All the mystery to read,

For it was her tender promptings,
   Brought about this wondrous deed.
So on Angel wings uprising,
   Spake she forth in joyful strain:
"Thorns are now preferred to flowers,
   Peace and glory spring from pain."

---

## MAY SONG.

Golden days and silver nights,
Fill the soul with pure delights;
We are happy, let us sing
To the mother of our King.
      Chorus.
Virgin, hear our fond appeal,
At thy shrine we humbly kneel,
Giving homage every day,
In the lovely month of May.

Freely now the waters flow,
Laughing roses bud and blow;
Beauty shines on every sod,
Lighted by the smile of God.
      Chorus.

Bigger stars appear on high
Shining in a bluer sky;

Sunny rays so scarce before,
Now in torrents stream and pour.
CHORUS.

Every hill and every sward
'Neath the footsteps of the Lord,
Wears a greener, fresher grace;
Gladness reigns in every place.
CHORUS.

While the earth and sky rejoice,
Let us raise our thankful voice,
Blessing God by night and day,
In the lovely month of May.
CHORUS.

## THE ALTAR.

WHERE the holy Altar stands,
Unseen Angels come in bands
Bearing censers in their hands.
 Watch and ward they nightly keep,
 While the dewy heavens weep—
 While forgetful mortals sleep.

And our faithful Sires now dead,
Bending knee and bowing head,
At the Altar railing prayed.

Poured their hearts before the Lord,
Vowing to confess his word
E'en beneath the tyrant's sword.

There we took the Christian name,
Felt the Holy Spirit's flame,
There the Lord our food became.
    There to second life we sprung;
    When our passing-bell is rung,
    There our requiem shall be sung.

Ancient Bethlem's chosen grot,
Calvary's awful height, were not
Holier than this holy spot.
    Hither let us come, and meet
    Vows of courage to repeat,
    Kneeling at the Saviour's feet.

Happy silver, happy gold,
Which the artists mix and mould,
His dear members to enfold.
    Happy Lamp, before the shrine,
    May my fervor burn and shine
    Like that steady flame of thine!

Happy lights and flowers that pay
Night by night, and day by day,
All their little life away—

May their fate my soul betide,
Near my Jesus to abide,
Love and languish by his side.

## ADORO TE.*

I bow before thee, unseen Deity,
That 'neath these forms hast truly hidden thee;
My heart is wholly subject to thy sway,
For in thy love divine it melts away.

The sight and touch and taste are here deceived,
But hearing can be fearlessly believed,
I hold to what was taught us by our Lord,
Naught can be truer than his own true word.

The God alone was on the Cross concealed,
But here the man as well is unrevealed,
Yet both confessing with a firm belief,
I breathe the prayer of the repentant thief.

Thy wounds with Thomas I claim not to see,
But as the Lord my God I worship thee;
Increase my faith by graces from above,
And fill my very soul with hope and love.

* From the Latin of St. Thomas Aquinas.

Memorial of the Saviour's parting breath,
O living bread that savest man from death,
My soul implores that God to her may give
The grace forever on thy sweets to live.

As feeds the Pelican her helpless brood,
Lord! feed us sinners with thy precious blood
Of which a single drop in mercy spilt,
Can ransom all the world from all its guilt.

O Jesus, whom so dimly I discern,
Grant me the happiness for which I yearn:
Thy face unveiled to see in all its light
And feast forever on the blissful sight.
Amen.

## THE BROKEN PROMISE.

The vows which I have spoken,
   Were spoken, Lord, to thee;
The promises I've broken
   Were told on bended knee.
'Twas not to earthly chief or king,
   That fealty was sworn by me,
The vows which I have spoken,
   Were made, O Lord, to thee,
     O Lord, O Lord,
   Were made to thee.

The vows which I have spoken,
  Were spoken at thy shrine,
There stands the Cross, a token
  Of might and grace divine.
Give ear unto my earnest prayer,
  And save this erring soul of mine,
No mercy can avail me,
  No might, O Lord, but thine,
  O Lord, O Lord,
  No might but thine.

## THE HEREAFTER.

Forth a stern decree hath issued,
  It is sanctioned from on high,
Every child that's born of Adam
  He shall one day surely die.
Gilded dome and naked rafter
  Both shall echo to the call,
The Hereafter! The Hereafter!
  We are hastening to it all.

In the flush of recent triumph,
  We may lay the warning by,
In the ardor of our strivings
  May refuse to think it nigh.

We may drown the thought in laughter,
　　In life's crowded banquet hall,
The Hereafter! The Hereafter!
　　We are hastening to it all.

Troops of friends may gather round us,
　　Cheer our toil with loving eye,
Enemies with base deception
　　Turn our best-laid schemes awry;
Death may pierce with sudden shaft, or
　　Age may slowly spread our pall,
The Hereafter! The Hereafter!
　　We are hastening to it all.

When the fatal knell is tolling,
　　Man may be unfit to die,
Or the ready soul may gladly
　　From this vale of sorrow fly;
Virtue on light wings may waft her,
　　Sin may press her in her fall,
The Hereafter! The Hereafter!
　　We are hastening to it all.

## A DIRGE.

LET a pious prayer be said,
For the spirits of the dead,

That their sufferings may cease,
That they soon may rest in peace.
  CHORUS.
Hear us, Father, while we pray
For the friends now passed away,
Show them mercy, grant them rest,
In the City of the Blest.
  Miserere—Miserere!

If a blemish or a stain
Should upon the soul remain,
Until cleansed it cannot rise
To the gates of Paradise.
CHORUS—Hear us, Father, while we pray, &c.

But your prayer for those you love,
Rises to the Lord above,
By their Saviour's holy name
They are rescued from the flame.
CHORUS—Hear us, Father, while we pray, &c.

## THE RESURRECTION.

CHRIST is risen from the dead,
Risen, as he truly said;
Praise the Lord with grateful voice,
Bless his name, Rejoice, Rejoice!

CHORUS.
Resurrexit,
Sicut dixit,
Alleluia, Alleluia,
Allelnia, Allelnia.

Angels clad in snowy white,
Coming from the realms of light,
Bid us sing with grateful voice,
Bid us all Rejoice, Rejoice!
  CHORUS—Resurrexit, &c.

Man was but a slave before,
Man is free for evermore;
Heaven and earth with grateful voice,
Bid us all Rejoice, Rejoice!
  CHORUS—Resurrexit, &c.

## THE GUERDON.

ZEALOUS for the honor
  Of the Lord above,
May I serve the donor,
  For his gifts of love.
Give not earthly pleasure,
  Riches, or renown,

Give me for my treasure,
  Lord, thyself alone.
    O Lord!
    Thyself alone.

Saints and Martyrs holy
  In ecstatic thought,
Dwell upon thee solely,
  Value self as naught,
Seeking through life's story,
  And when life is done,
Seeking for their glory,
  Lord, thyself alone.
    O Lord!
    Thyself alone.

Angels see thee clearly
  In the blessed choirs,
They by wishing merely
  Gain their heart's desires.
But their bliss is never
  Severed from thy own,
And they love forever,
  Lord, thyself alone.
    O Lord!
    Thyself alone.

## EMBLEMS OF LIFE.

I passed a rose at early morn,
  'Twas blooming fresh and fair,
When evening came a naked thorn
  Was all that met me there.
    And then my spirit spoke to me,
      And thus to me did say:
    "There is a lesson here for thee,
      Thus life doth pass away."

I heard a silver lute that kept
  True time to loving words;
But soon the hand of madness swept,
  And broke the trembling chords.
    And then my spirit spoke to me, &c.

I saw great domes and spires of cloud
  Lit up with purple light;
But suddenly the wind blew loud
  And swept them into night.
    And then my spirit spoke to me, &c.

I learned that on a sunny beach
  A marble city grew;
But now its silent ruins bleach
  Beneath the waters blue.
    And then my spirit spoke to me, &c.

## THE WORSHIP OF NATURE.
(Music by PIETRO PAOLICCHI.)

There's worship where the roses bloom,
  Where violets are found,
Among the flowers that bow at morn
  With shining dew-drops crowned.
And all the blossoms, red and white,
  That scent the leafy grove,
They too proclaim their Maker's name,
  And thank Him for his love.

There's worship where the merry birds
  Are flying o'er the plain;
And where they peck the berries bright,
  Adown the shady lane.
And 'midst the golden grain below,
  Or blushing fruit above,
They, too, proclaim their Maker's name,
  And thank Him for his love.

There's worship in the foaming brook
  That down the mountain pours;
And on the blue lake feathering
  The boatman's lifted oars.
Where waters court the cooling shade,
  And where they gaily rove,

They, too, proclaim their Maker's name,
  And thank Him for his love.

There's worship 'mid the sober herds
  That browse 'neath aged oaks,
Along the grassy meadows where
  The shepherds tend their flocks.
And where the fishes, great and small,
  Beneath old ocean move,
They, too, proclaim their Maker's name,
  And thank Him for his love.

There's worship 'mid the countless worlds
  That roll through boundless space;
The hand that fashioned all the stars,
  Guides each one in its race.
These works of God pray not like man,
  But while his might they prove,
Bid man proclaim their Maker's name,
  And thank Him for his love.

## THE CHERISHED HOPE.

AIR—*Ach wenn du wärst mein eigen.*

THE Hope which I have cherished,
  It was a gift of thine,
Though dreams of joy have perished,
  This Hope was ever mine.

The bud of promise morn bestows,
At night is oft a withered rose.
The Hope which I have cherished,
  It was a gift of thine,
  A gift, a gift, O Lord, of thine!

The hope which I have cherished,
  It was a gift from thee,
My friends have flown or perished,
  But thou art true to me.
The stars that gemmed my journey's dawn
Have failed me as I journeyed on.
The Hope which I have cherished,
  It was a gift from thee,
  A gift, a gift, O Lord, from thee.

## ANTIPHON FROM COMPLIN.

### First Chorus.

Salva nos Domine vigilantes,
Custodi nos dormientes.

### Second Chorus.

Save us, Father, when we wake,
Guard us while our rest we take.

### First Chorus.

Ut vigilemus cum Christo,
Et requiescamus in pace.   Amen.

### Second Chorus.

May we watch with Christ, and then
Sleep the sleep of peace.   Amen.

---

## NEAPOLITAN MARINER'S HYMN.

#### Air.—Santa Lucia.

Dark clouds are over us
  Stealthily creeping,
Wild billows threaten us
  Angrily leaping.
Hear us, we fly to thee,
  Mother of Purity,
            Sancta Maria.

Through storm-clouds tenderly
  The blue sky smiling
Beams on us lovingly
  All dread beguiling.
Hear us, we fly to thee,
  Mother of Purity,
            Sancta Maria.

In the drear solitude
Hope's form appearing
Shines white and beautiful,
Our weak hearts cheering.
Hear us, we fly to thee,
  Mother of Purity,
              Sancta Maria.

Now to the Mariner
  Fear is a stranger,
Mary his Patroness
  Saves him from danger.
Hear us, we fly to thee,
  Mother of Purity,
              Sancta Maria.

Saved from the dangerous
  Wrath of the billow,
Now the poor Mariner
  Seeketh his pillow.
Hear us, we fly to thee,
  Mother of Purity,
              Sancta Maria.

## THE HAPPY DAY.
### Music by P. Rondinella,

This day is a day of rejoicing;
Let ev'ry dull memory vanish,
Let each one his misery banish,
   And be like the day bright and fair.
Pour out your full hearts in a chorus,
A chorus of innocent gladness;
Away with all sorrow and sadness,
   Away with all troublesome care.

All Nature pours forth a thanksgiving
When sunlight the dull earth is flooding,
And thousands of flowers are budding
   Beneath the light footsteps of Spring;
And now that our Father in heaven,
His prodigal children caressing,
Receives us and gives us a blessing,
   We too will be happy and sing.

This life is not evermore gloomy
To those who are manfully coping,
For while they are fearing and hoping
   The victory comes from above.
And when we think the Almighty
O'erwhelms us with sorrowful feeling,
In truth He is only revealing
   A proof of His goodness and love.

This day is a day of rejoicing,
Away with all weakly repining—
The sun of past ages is shining
　Above us in glory to-day;
Past trials are gone and forgotten,
The present is free from all sorrow,
And trusting in God for to-morrow,
　We'll happily sing while we may.

## TWILIGHT MUSINGS.
### MUSIC BY P. RONDINELLA.

TWILIGHT is a witching hour,
　Let its grey and purple wing
Gently spread its magic power
　O'er my senses while I sing.
Twilight gleaneth tender musings
　From the new-mown fields of thought,
Art in graceful sheaves will bind them,
　Lest they wilt and come to naught.

Twilight mirrors forth to Poets
　Dreamy views of calm delight,
Sweeter quiet, grander silence,
　Deeper shade and broader light,
Visions of the young and lovely
　Borne away to early graves,
Visions of the strong and fearless
　Wrecked in Ocean's mossy caves.

Pearly dew-beads o'er the meadow
   Sown in rich profusion lie,
While the fire-fly's ruby kindles
   Like a torch-light swung on high.
Seen no more, the thrush and linnet
   Settle on their downy nest,
But the robin's plaintive numbers
   Lull the whispering wood to rest.

Lo! athwart the trembling Ocean
   Stretches forth a bridge of gold,
Is its shining pathway ever
   Trod by feet of earthly mould?
Are the souls of Saints departing,
   Led by Angels o'er that way,
Up to yon half-open portals
   Blazing with eternal day?

Now the languid flowers are sleeping
   Birds are slumb'ring on their nest,
Heaven's broad cathedral windows
   Darken in the cloudy West;
And a deeper haze is spreading,
   Spreading o'er the fading scene,
Stars are peeping out in heaven—
   Day is dead—and Night is Queen.

# DEFINITIONS

AND

# AIDS TO MEMORY

FOR THE

## CATECHISM;

BEING

A CATECHISM IN RHYME.

BY

REV. DR. CUMMINGS,
Pastor of St. Stephen's Church, New York.

---

NEW YORK:
D. & J. SADLIER,
31 Barclay Street.

Entered according to Act of Congress, in the year 1862,
BY J. W. CUMMINGS,
In the Clerk's Office of the District Court of the United States, for the Southern District of New York.

# DEFINITIONS
### AND
# AIDS TO MEMORY
## FOR THE CATECHISM.

---

## ACTS OF FAITH, HOPE, CHARITY, AND CONTRITION.

#### ACT OF FAITH.

GREAT God! whatever through Thy Church
    Thou teachest to be true,
I firmly do believe it all,
    And shall confess it too.
Thou never canst deceived be,
    Thou never canst deceive,
For Thou art truth itself, and Thou
    Dost tell me to believe.

### ACT OF HOPE.

My God! I firmly hope in Thee,
    For Thou art great and good,
And gavest us Thine only Son
    To die upon the rood.
I hope through him for grace to live
    As Thy commandments teach,
And through Thy mercy when I die,
    The joys of heaven to reach.

### ACT OF LOVE.

With all my heart, and soul, and strength,
    I love Thee, O my Lord,
For Thou art perfect, and all things
    Were made by Thy blest Word.
Like me to Thine own image made,
    My neighbor Thou didst make,
And as I love myself, I love
    My neighbor for Thy sake.

### ACT OF CONTRITION.

Most holy God! my very soul
    With grief sincere is moved,
Because I have offended Thee,
    Whom I should e'er have loved.

Forgive me, Father! I am now,
　Resolved to sin no more,
And by thy holy grace to shun
　What made me sin before.

## THE TEN COMMANDMENTS OF GOD.

### I.

I am thy God and Sovereign Lord,
Naught else must be as God adored.

### II.

All sacred things thy reverence claim,
Take not in vain God's holy name.

### III.

Keep holy every Sabbath-day,
And do not work, but rest and pray.

### IV.

All honor to thy Parents pay,
Nor their just wishes disobey.

### V.

Treat all as kindly as you can,
Kill not, nor hate your fellow-man.

### VI.

From lewd temptations turn with haste,
And never do an act unchaste.

### VII.

Give what is due to every one,
And take not what is not thine own.

### VIII.

Speak always what is true and fair,
Lie not, nor e'er false witness bear.

### IX.

Preserve thy fancy free from stain,
And lustful thoughts ne'er entertain.

### X.

Be just in purpose and design,
And covet not what is not thine.

---

## THE SIX PRECEPTS OF THE CHURCH.

### I.

Let not a Feast or Sunday pass
Without once hearing Holy Mass.

### II.

Whene'er the Church shall so ordain,
Keep fast, or from flesh meat abstain.

### III.

Make every twelvemonth once at least
A good Confession to your Priest.

#### IV.

Each year, at Easter time at least,
Approach the Eucharistic feast.

#### V.

The Priest must by the people live,
And you to him your mite should give.

#### VI.

The rules for Christian marriage made
Must be respected and obeyed.

---

## GRACE.

GRACE is the light God gives the mind,
That we the truth may surely find—
Grace is the strength he gives free will,
His holy precepts to fulfill.

---

## A SACRAMENT.

An outward sign of inward grace
  By Christ ordained and made—
A mystic rite by which his grace
  Is to our souls conveyed.

# THE SEVEN SACRAMENTS.

### I.

We are cleansed from sin original
    In Baptism's holy waters;
We are chosen heirs of heaven, and made
    God's happy sons and daughters.

### II.

We are rendered perfect Christians when
    We are signed in Confirmation,
And God the Holy Ghost gives strength
    To conquer all temptation.

### III.

Christ present in the Eucharist
    To worship we are bidden;
Beneath the forms of bread and wine
    The Lord is truly hidden.

### IV.

All sins that after Baptism
    A man may have committed,
If he is sorry from his heart
    By Penance are remitted.

### V.

The Last Anointing heals the flesh,
   New life and strength imparting;
Or else insures a happy death
   To souls from earth departing.

### VI.

In Holy Order Priests receive
   Their heavenly commission,
With grace to worthily fulfill
   The duties of their mission.

### VII.

In Matrimony, Christians are
   As man and wife united,
Receiving grace from God to keep
   The faith which they have plighted.

---

## SEVEN CORPORAL WORKS OF MERCY.

VISIT, give ransom, raiment, drink, and bread,
Shelter the homeless, and inter the dead.

---

## SEVEN SPIRITUAL WORKS OF MERCY.

TEACH, counsel, soothe, correct, forgive, and bear,
Think of the living and the dead in prayer.

## THE SEVEN DEADLY SINS.

PRIDE is inordinate esteem that one
Has for himself, or what by him is done.*

Avarice is the immoderate love of gain
Which we have got, or which we would obtain.

Lust means all impure pleasure, be it sought
By look, by word, by action, or by thought.

Anger is passion quick and violent,
That moves the will some grievance to resent.

Gluttony is the abuse of drink and meat;
It does not eat to live, it lives to eat.

Envy is sorrow at another's gain,
Or it is pleasure at another's pain,

Sloth is a cold disrelish that withdraws
The sluggish heart from God and from his laws.

## THE EIGHT BEATITUDES.

BLESSED the poor in spirit, they are heirs
To wealth untold, for heaven itself is theirs.

---

\* (Vanity means the inordinate desire
That other folks may praise us or admire.)

Blessed the meek, for without strife their hand
Shall be victorious, and possess the land.

Blessed are they that mourn, for God one day
Will comfort them, and wipe their tears away.

Blessed who hunger and who thirst, unskilled
In wiles, for justice, for they shall be filled.

Blessed the merciful, they shall obtain
The mercy which they grant their fellow-men.

Blessed the clean of heart, for they shall see
The Lord in all his cloudless purity.

Blessed are all peace-makers kind and mild—
Children of God they shall be justly styled.

Blessed are they that suffer in the right,
For heaven's kingdom shall their cares requite.

## CANTICLE ON THE BLESSED SACRAMENT.

Hail! most holy Sacrament
Where God is our aliment.
In thee Jesus we behold—
His own tongue this truth has told.

In the Eucharistic bread,
With his flesh our souls are fed.
Who can doubt the word he spoke,
When that mystic bread he broke?

Man was lost in sin and shame—
To redeem him Jesus came;
Came the Father's equal Son,
Our frail nature to put on.

Son of man and Son of God,
Over Judah's plains he trod.
Blessings round his footsteps fall—
Grace and truth he gives to all.

Came that ever-blessed night,
When, concealing all his might,
To be slaughtered by his foes
Like a helpless lamb he goes.

But before the fearful hour,
When was loosened hell's dark power,
He drew closer to his heart
Those with whom he had to part.

See! around the sacred board
Sit the twelve and their own Lord!
Who the flames of love can tell
That within his bosom dwell?

Hearken to his loving voice!
Hark! and let thy soul rejoice—
Pledged to thee as well as those
Is the gift he now bestows.

Ended is the obscure rite
Which belonged to Jewish night.
Shadowy figures now give way
To the splendor of new day.

Holding in his hands the bread,
"This my body is," he said;
"This the body, real, true,
I shall immolate for you."

Holding forth what now was wine,
"Take," he says, "this blood of mine—
Living blood which soon shall be
Shed, the world from sin to free.

Eat of this, my very flesh,
With my blood your souls refresh;
When my earthly course is run,
Do ye what I now have done."

'Twas the Word Divine that spoke!
He whose order could evoke
Out of nothing's dark abyss
All that was and all that is.

At his voice the glorious sun
First began his course to run.
He, too, summoned every star,
And all answered, "Here we are."

In the heavens and on the earth,
All things owe to him their birth.
He alone their being gave—
He can change, destroy, or save.

Ages come and ages go—
Age or change he cannot know.
And the word that spoke his will
Stands forever changeless still.

And the Apostles, ever true,
Did that which he bade them do—
Blessed the sacred bread and wine,
Changed to elements divine.

When before your vision pass
The dread mysteries of the Mass,
Jesus Christ is present still,
That same wonder to fulfill.

At the sacred Altar-stone
Stands the Priest, but not alone,
For the voice of God is heard
In the consecrating word.

## FOR THE CATECHISM.

Jesus did this promise make—
Made it for his mercy's sake;
And his word will faithful stay,
Never, never pass away.

Thus to flesh is changed the bread,
Wine into the blood he shed.
Lacketh he nor power nor will
What he promised to fulfill.

Heresy and fatal pride
May this mystery deride;
We faith's humble offering bring
To our Saviour and our King.

Jesus, who upon the cross
Saved us from eternal loss—
Jesus, living God on high,
In the Sacrament is nigh.

Adoration, honor, love,
Let us give to God above.
Chiefly let our praise be told
For the gift our altars hold.

[I am happy in being permitted to adorn my book with the foregoing admirable Canticle, composed by one of the most learned and distinguished ecclesiastics in America, and communicated to me by the author, to testify his approval of my exertions for the benefit of our children.]

## THE SEVEN GIFTS OF THE HOLY GHOST.

Spirit of Holiness
  Come from above,
Grant us the sevenfold
  Gift of thy love.

*Wisdom* points out to us
  Heaven's true worth;
None but vain happiness
  Springs from this earth.
        Spirit of Holiness, &c.

*Intellect* teaches us
  Even from youth,
Rightly to penetrate
  God's holy Truth.
        Spirit of Holiness, &c.

*Counsel* throws plentiful
  Light on our path,
Scatters our enemies,
  Baffles their wrath.
        Spirit of Holiness, &c.

*Fortitude* girdeth on
  Arms for the fight,

Making us warriors
  True to the right.
      Spirit of Holiness, &c.

*Knowledge* weighs good and ill
  Mingled by Doubt,
Goodness is treasured up,
  Evil cast out.
      Spirit of Holiness, &c.

*Godliness* pleasantly
  Leads us to do
What we have learned to be
  Noble and true.
      Spirit of Holiness, &c.

*Fear of the Lord* in us
  Trains us to die
Rather than break the law.
  Of the Most High.
      Spirit of Holiness, &c.

## THE TWELVE FRUITS OF THE HOLY GHOST.

Holy Spirit, in my bosom
  Plant and foster blessed fruit—
In pure hearts it springeth ever
  From thy grace as from its root.

*Charity* sincere and earnest
  In the service of the Lord
Makes us fear to disobey him,
  Makes us love to keep his word,
          Holy Spirit, &c.

*Joy* inclines us still with pleasure
  To obey our Father's will,
Of the calm delights of virtue,
  So we come to drink our fill.
          Holy Spirit, &c.

*Peace* amid the toil and trouble
  Brought upon our race by sin,
Spite of angry storms around us,
  Keeps a tranquil mind within.
          Holy Spirit, &c.

*Patience* 'mid our varied trials
  Saves us from a peevish mood,
Leads us e'en to view affliction
  As a mercy and a good.
          Holy Spirit, &c.

'Tis *Benignity* that makes us
  Bear no malice in the mind,
Makes us slow in judging others,
  In forgiving prompt and kind.
          Holy Spirit, &c.

*Goodness* keeps us ever ready
   To perform a kindly deed,
To feel pity for another,
   And to help him in his need.
        Holy Spirit, &c.

*Longanimity* inspires us
   With endurance for the fight,
Trains us never to grow weary
   In the cause of truth and right.
        Holy Spirit, &c.

*Mildness* forms an even temper,
   Keeps rebellious passion low.
And by sweet and gentle manners
   Wins the love of friend and foe.
        Holy Spirit, &c.

*Faith* when we have made a promise
   Keeps us to that promise true,
Makes us honest in fulfilling
   What we pledge our word to do.
        Holy Spirit, &c.

*Modesty* restrains the Christian
   From all proud and boastful ways;
In his speech it makes him careful
   Not to utter selfish praise.
        Holy Spirit, &c.

*Continence* by steady combat
Holds in check the carnal mind,
Makes it keep the path of duty
By the law of God defined.
  Holy Spirit, &c.

*Chastity* creates within us
Perfect love for purity,
Till the soul, grown like the angels,
E'en from truant thought is free.
  Holy Spirit, &c.

## THE FOUR GREAT ENDS FOR WHICH HOLY MASS IS OFFERED.

### I.
To worship at Jehovah's throne,
Adoring Him, and Him alone.

### II.
To sue for pardon, and implore
The help of God to sin no more.

### III.
To beg Him that his holy grace
May be our guide in every place.

### IV.
To thank and bless the Lord for all
His countless favors, great and small.

## FOUR LAST THINGS TO BE REMEMBERED.

PREPARE for Death—you'll surely die one day;
But when, or where, or how, no man can say.

Fear Judgment—to a wise and mighty Lord
You must account for thought, and deed, and word.

Remember Hell to shun it—dark despair,
Fire, and the worm that never dies, are there.

Look up to Heaven!—if you are firm and true
In serving God, its joys are all for you.

---

## THE SEVEN SORROWS OF THE B. V. M.

### 1.

By Simeon old the future's told
  Of God's incarnate Word,
And Mary's care is to prepare
  Her heart for sorrow's sword.

Mother! our sins with seven swords
  Have pierced thy sacred breast,
But in thy presence and thy Lord's
  All sin we now detest.

2.

Rude soldiers stain fair Bethlehem's plain
  With children's rosy gore,
Warned from on high his parents fly
  With Christ to Egypt's shore.
                    Mother, &c.

3.

Through streets and ways Our Lady strays,
  Till three long days are done;
All sorrow past, she then at last
  Embraces her dear Son.
                    Mother, &c.

4.

Our Lady hears how Jesus bears
  His cross—oh, bitter load!
With heart resigned she hastes to find,
  And meet him on the road.
                    Mother, &c.

5.

Mount Calvary's brow is gained, and now
  The Lord they crucify;
While to fulfill the Almighty's will
  His mother stands near by.
                    Mother, &c.

### 6.

With reverent care his friends repair
　　To take the body down;
In death He sleeps, his mother weeps,
　　And shares his thorny crown.
　　　　　　　　Mother, &c.

### 7.

They reach the cave, and in its grave
　　The Saviour's body lies;
His mother's grief finds no relief
　　Till from the dead He rise.
　　　　　　　　Mother, &c.

## ASPIRATION.

A spirit sent by Satan, Mother,
　　Tempts me to go astray—
Send one of thy good angels, Mother,
　　To drive him far away.

## THE FOURTEEN STATIONS OF THE CROSS.

### I.

The Son of God came down from heaven,
　　Upon the earth to dwell,
And man condemns to cruel death
　　The heart that loved him well.

Thou goest forth, O Blessed Lord,
  To suffer death for me,
And I too wish for thee to live—
  I wish to die for thee.

II.

He taketh up his heavy Cross,
  And bears the crushing load;
And as he meekly journeys on,
  His blood bedews the road.

   Thou goest forth, &c.

III.

Rude soldiers press and goad him on,
  And straiten him around,
And now, beneath his weighty Cross,
  He falls upon the ground.

   Thou goest forth, &c.

IV.

His Mother hastens forth to join
  The Son she loved so well;
Their glances meet, their hearts are filled
  With grief no tongue can tell.

   Thou goest forth, &c.

### V.

They fear the Saviour may expire
　Beneath his heavy load,
And Simon is compelled to bear
　His Cross along the road.

　　　　　Thou goest forth, &c.

### VI.

A Jewish woman wipes his face—
　Her pity to reward,
Upon her veil remains impressed
　An image of the Lord.

　　　　　Thou goest forth, &c.

### VII.

The Saviour falls a second time,
　Oppressed with bitter pain;
The soldiers force him to arise,
　And journey on again.

　　　　　Thou goest forth, &c.

### VIII.

The Daughters of Jerusalem
　Bewail his cruel fate;
He bids them for their children weep,
　Before it is too late.

　　　　　Thou goest forth, &c.

## IX.

He's urged to move with quicker step;
  His blood in torrents flows;
Again, again he falls to earth,
  Beneath their cruel blows.
                Thou goest forth, &c.

## X.

The soldiers strip with violence
  The garments from his flesh,
And every wound he had received
  Is made to bleed afresh.
                Thou goest forth, &c.

## XI.

They lay him down upon the Cross;
  They nail his hands and feet;
The Cross is raised, and he is left
  His coming death to meet.
                Thou goest forth, &c.

## XII.

Three hours of agony had passed
  Since he was crucified;
His work was done, his hour was come—
  He bowed his head and died.
                Thou goest forth, &c.

### XIII.

Now his disciples come and take
    The body from the Cross;
His Mother folds it in her arms,
    And mourns her bitter loss.

        Thou goest forth, &c.

### XIV.

His followers bear him to the tomb,
    Prepared with pious care,
Then silently depart, and leave
    The sacred body there.

        Thou goest forth, &c.

**THE END.**

# SONGS

FOR

## CATHOLIC SCHOOLS,

AND

### THE CATECHISM IN RHYME.

BY

REV. DR. CUMMINGS.

---

MUSIC.

# INTRODUCTORY REMARKS,

### BY

### SIGNOR SPERANZA.

---

WHEN I had the honor of being chosen by the Rev. Dr. Cummings to work with him in preparing this collection for the public, I found myself limited in composition to short musical phrases, and a very brief compass of notes, the melodies being intended for children. Children, even in large numbers, and entirely ignorant of music, will easily acquire them. The method I would recommend for teaching them is the *echo* system. It is practised in the following manner:

The teacher sings one phrase himself, then, with a tap or little stroke of a ruler, gives the signal that the children are to repeat immediately the phrase he has sung. If they make any mistake, the teacher will repeat the phrase until they learn it well. One phrase being learned, the next will be taken up, the teacher singing and the children following immediately at the signal as before, until phrases enough are learned to form a period. The teacher will go over the phrases already learned, and the children will repeat first two phrases at a time, and then four, until the whole period is learned. One period being learned, the others will follow, until the whole piece is sung correctly.

## INTRODUCTORY REMARKS.

To obtain good results from this method, the following rules must be carefully observed:

1. Strict discipline must be maintained among the scholars.

2. The person teaching must sing with a distinct, decided, and clean enunciation of both notes and words, bringing out more expressly those notes which the scholars seem to have most difficulty in seizing with precision.

3. The children must be trained and compelled to sing always *sotto-voce*, until they have learned well the piece they are studying.

4. It is of the greatest importance that the scholars shall not begin to sing until the signal is given by a tap of the ruler, when they must begin immediately, and all together.

The habit of singing very piano while learning has an excellent effect on children, who are so organized that it is with the greatest difficulty they can be induced to pass into the upper register, or the *voce di testa*. If they are called upon to sing an ascending scale, they keep on as long as the lower range, the *voce di petto*, and *voce di mezzo* will allow, but when they get up to the high notes they either stop, or else force the voice to a scream. To allow them to go on in this way would put them out of breath, and might do them serious injury, ruining their voices perhaps forever.

DOMENICO SPERANZA.

# Songs for Catholic Schools.

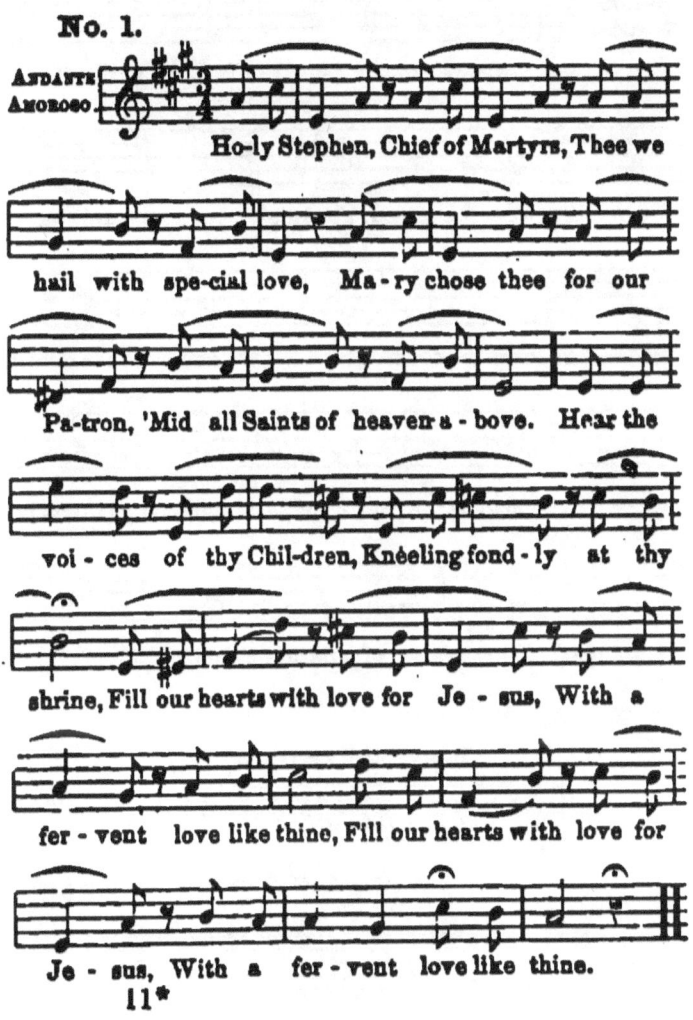

# SONGS FOR CATHOLIC SCHOOLS.

## No. 2.

There's music in the bubbling rill, That

fro - lics o'er the mead, That makes the silver dai - sy

bloom, And laves the nodding reed. There's music in the gentle

breeze, That whispers thro' the wood, And softly sings to mortal

things, The praise of nature's God.

## No. 3.

The Messenger An-gel de-scend-ing at

night, Chased si - lence and sha-dow with mu - sic and

SONGS FOR CATHOLIC SCHOOLS. 3

light, The shepherds of Beth-le-hem heard on the

plain, The Mes-sen-ger An-gel, and this was his

una voce sola.
strain: "May peace be to mor-tals and glo-ry to

heaven, The Pro-mised of old to man-kind has been

given, Re-joice at the splendor that heralds his

birth, The Sa-viour, the Sa-viour has come up-on

tutti con gioja.
earth, The Saviour, the Saviour has come up-on earth."

No. 4.

ANDANTE
GRANDIOSO.

The earth, O Lord, re-joi-ces, And

4          SONGS FOR CATHOLIC SCHOOLS.

sings with glad acclaim A hymn of ma-ny voi-ces, In

hon-or of thy name. We join the hap-py chorus, That

hails the morning light, And bless the Lord that o'er us Kept

mancando.
lov-ing watch all night, all night, all night.

No. 5.

ANDANTINO
AMOROSO.

Hail Vir-gin of virgins, Thy praises we

sing, Thy throne is in heaven, Thy Son is its King.

The saints and the an-gels, Thy glo-ry pro-claim, All

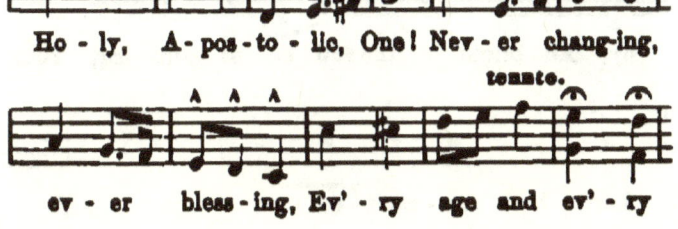

6 SONGS FOR CATHOLIC SCHOOLS.

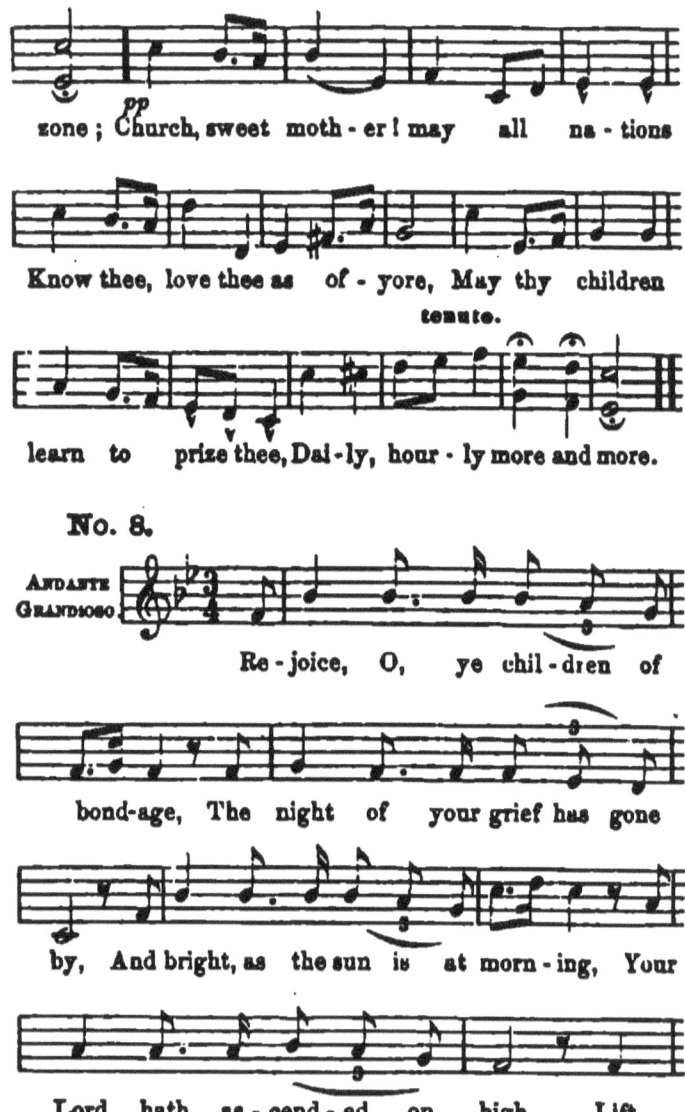

zone; Church, sweet moth-er! may all na-tions
Know thee, love thee as of-yore, May thy children
*tenuto.*
learn to prize thee, Dai-ly, hour-ly more and more.

No. 8.

ANDANTE
GRANDIOSO

Re-joice, O, ye chil-dren of
bond-age, The night of your grief has gone
by, And bright, as the sun is at morn-ing, Your
Lord hath as-cend-ed on high. Lift

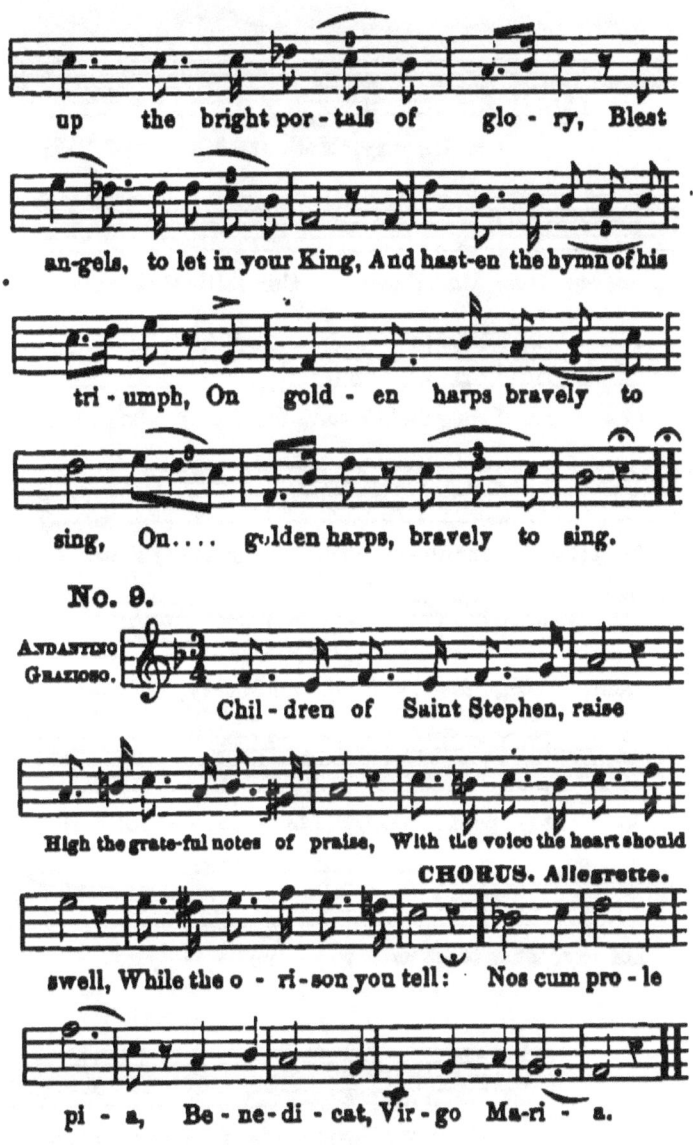

## No. 10.

*Grazioso.*

Oh, Ma-ry, Moth-er Ma-ry! We place our trust in thee— Our faith shall nev-er va-ry, Though weak the flesh may be; Too oft with steps un-wa-ry, From du-ty's path we've bent, Oh, Ma-ry, Moth-er Ma-ry, Thou teach us to re-pent, Oh, Ma-ry, Moth-er Ma-ry, Thou teach us to re-pent.

## No. 11.

*Andantino.*

When our Saviour wished to prove, All the

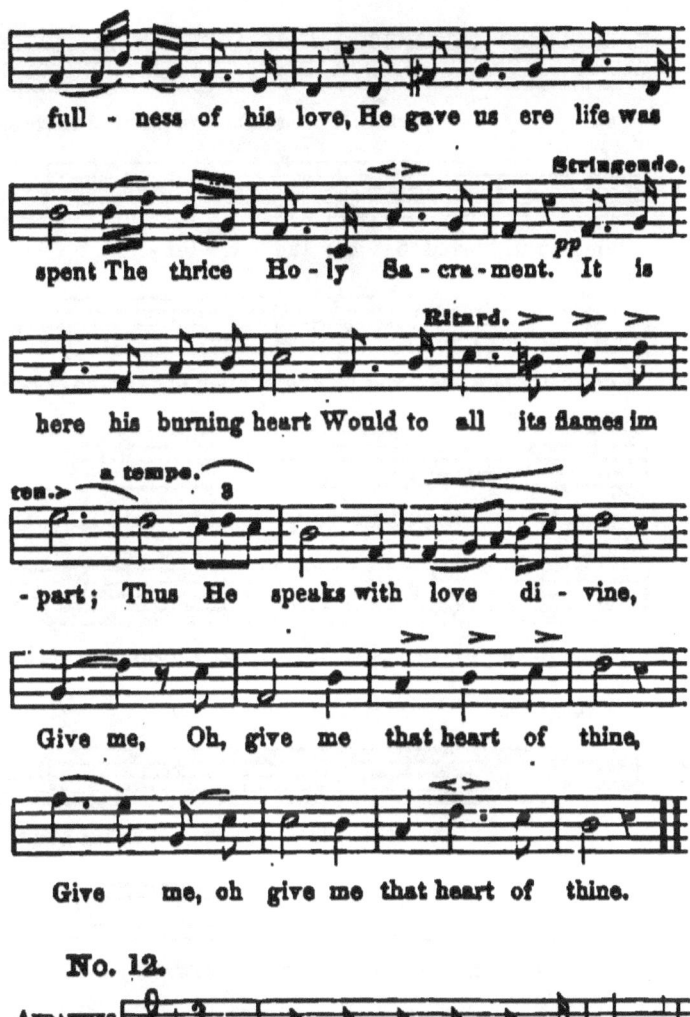

10  SONGS FOR CATHOLIC SCHOOLS.

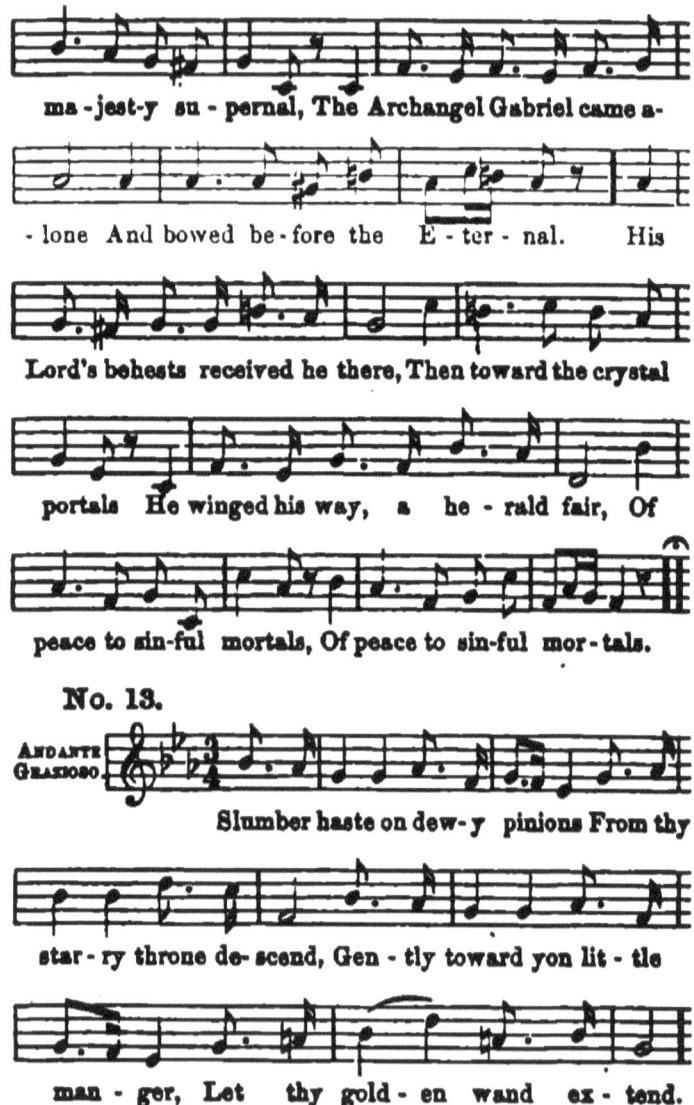

ma-jest-y su-pernal, The Archangel Gabriel came a-
- lone And bowed be-fore the E-ter-nal.  His
Lord's behests received he there, Then toward the crystal
portals He winged his way, a he-rald fair, Of
peace to sin-ful mortals, Of peace to sin-ful mor-tals.

No. 13.

ANDANTE GRAZIOSO.

Slumber haste on dew-y pinions From thy
star-ry throne de-scend, Gen-tly toward yon lit-tle
man-ger, Let thy gold-en wand ex-tend.

12   SONGS FOR CATHOLIC SCHOOLS.

spotless Queen of Virgins, With shining lilies crowned, Grant

CHORUS.

we thy youthful daughters, May pure like thee be found.

### No. 15.

AFFETTUOSO.

From thy bright throne a - bove the

sky, Look down on us, O Moth - er

sweet, And smile up - on the gift which I Here

of - fer, kneel - ing at thy feet. O!

Moth - er of my God and mine, I've

brought some sim - ple flowers to - day, That they may bloom up - on thy shrine, The long, long hours that I'm a - way.

### No. 16.

ANDANTINO AMOROSO.

The Tear of In - no - cence how bright It gush - es from the eye, It wins the sym - pa - thy of men, The blessings of the sky. Be - fore the ten - der in - fant's tongue Has

# SONGS FOR CATHOLIC SCHOOLS.

learned to shape a sound, It tells with sim - ple e - lo-quence His lit - tle wants a - round.

## No. 17.

**ANDANTE SOSTENUTO.**

Spir- its that languish In cleansing fire, Great is your anguish As your de - sire.

We who could lend you Aid and re - lief,

Fail to be - friend you, Leave you to grief,

Fail to be - friend you, Leave you to grief.

SONGS FOR CATHOLIC SCHOOLS. 15

No. 18.

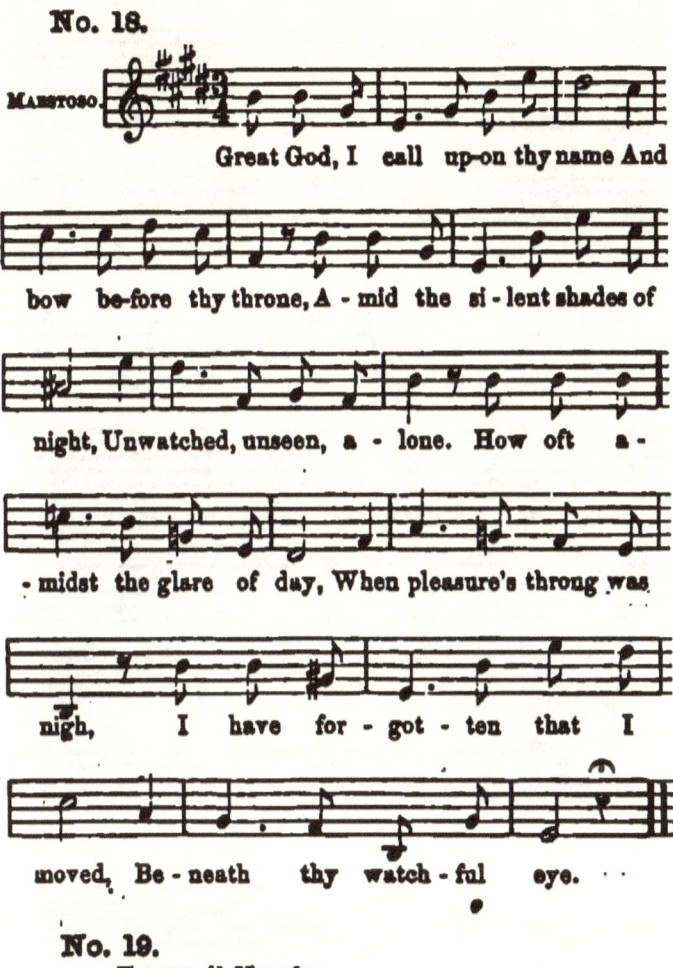

MAESTOSO.

Great God, I call up-on thy name And bow be-fore thy throne, A - mid the si - lent shades of night, Unwatched, unseen, a - lone. How oft a- -midst the glare of day, When pleasure's throng was nigh, I have for - got - ten that I moved, Be - neath thy watch - ful eye.

No. 19.

Tempo di Marcia.

MAESTOSO.

Ere Peace and Freedom hand in

16    SONGS FOR CATHOLIC SCHOOLS.

hand Went forth to bless this hap-py land, And make it their a - - bode. It was the foot-stool of a throne, But now no scep-tre here is known, No king is feared but God, No king is feared but God.

**No. 20.**

MAESTOSO.

Thy power, O Lord, is bound-less power, Thy love is bound-less love, And for that love and by that power Thou

18 SONGS FOR CATHOLIC SCHOOLS.

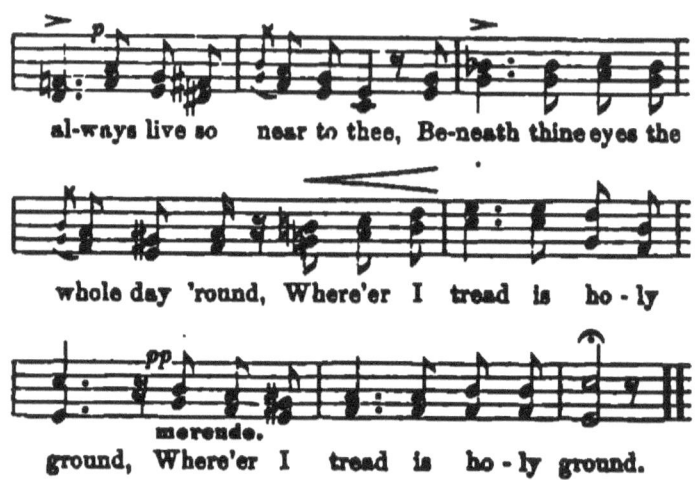

al-ways live so near to thee, Be-neath thine eyes the

whole day 'round, Where'er I tread is ho - ly

morendo.
ground, Where'er I tread is ho - ly ground.

### No. 23 and 24.

CANTABILE.

Haste, fond Mem'ry, thy vi - gor re-
Soul a - wak-en, in sad-ness why

- call - ing, Haste a - way to the val - leys and
lan - guish, Break a - way from thy fears and thy

mountains, Where the breeze o'er Ju - dea's bright
fet - ters, Feel the cour-age that rouses and

ho - - - ly, We march'd boldly thro' waste and thro'
*er - - - ror, And of dreams we grow fond - er and*

wild - wood, Sure to con - - quer, yet rea - dy to
*fond - er, If we call not, O Lord, on thy*

die. But our looks are de - ject - ed and
*power. While we pray ev' - ry vis - ion of*

low - ly, And thy ser - vants are bowed down with
*ter - ror Melts a - way like the dew - drops at*

sor - row; Shall the Cross and its war - riors to -
*morn-ing, And the wiles of the proud tempt - er*

- mor - row, Prove a scoff when the Pay-nim draw
*scorn - ing, We are free.. as in E - den's lost*

nigh? We re-mem-ber...... dear Lombar-dy's
bower. O, this world when.... it scat-ters its

moun-tains, Her...... vineyards, her fields rich in
flow-ers, When it gath-ers its tro-phies a-

glo-ry, Her fresh breez-es,.... her mur-mur-ing
-round me, May be-guile for.... a few fleet-ing

foun-tains, The green bow-ers that wave in her
hours,.... But my heart must be wretch-ed, or

land. Ah! fond mem-'ry, thou'rt scarce-ly a
thine. Then be-fore Death has spread his dark

bless-ing, Thou re-call-est our childhood's sweet
pin-ion, And the spell of its sha-dow has

24  SONGS FOR CATHOLIC SCHOOLS.

sto - ry, But we're roused from thy dream - y ca -
bound me, Let me bow to my Sa - viour's do -

- ress - ing, By the glow of the hot des - ert
- min - ion; Let his glo - ry or Cross still be

sand, By the glow of the hot des - ert
mine, Let his glo - ry, or Cross still be

sand, By the glow of the hot des - ert
mine, Let his glo - ry or Cross still be

sand, the hot des-ert sand, the hot des-ert sand.
mine, or Cross still be mine, or Cross still be mine.

No. 26.

ANDANTE
SOSTENUTO.

SOLO.

Almighty Sire! I'm dust, Unbounded

26　SONGS FOR CATHOLIC SCHOOLS.

-dore thee With the Fa - ther and the Word.

Thou art of the self - same na - ture

As the Father and the Son, E - qual - ly from both pro-

-ceed - ing, Thou dost bind them both in One.

No. 28.

Andante Religioso

Lord, when a sil - ver - y star

Gleams in the blue depths a - far,..

Thoughts come to me of thine eye,..

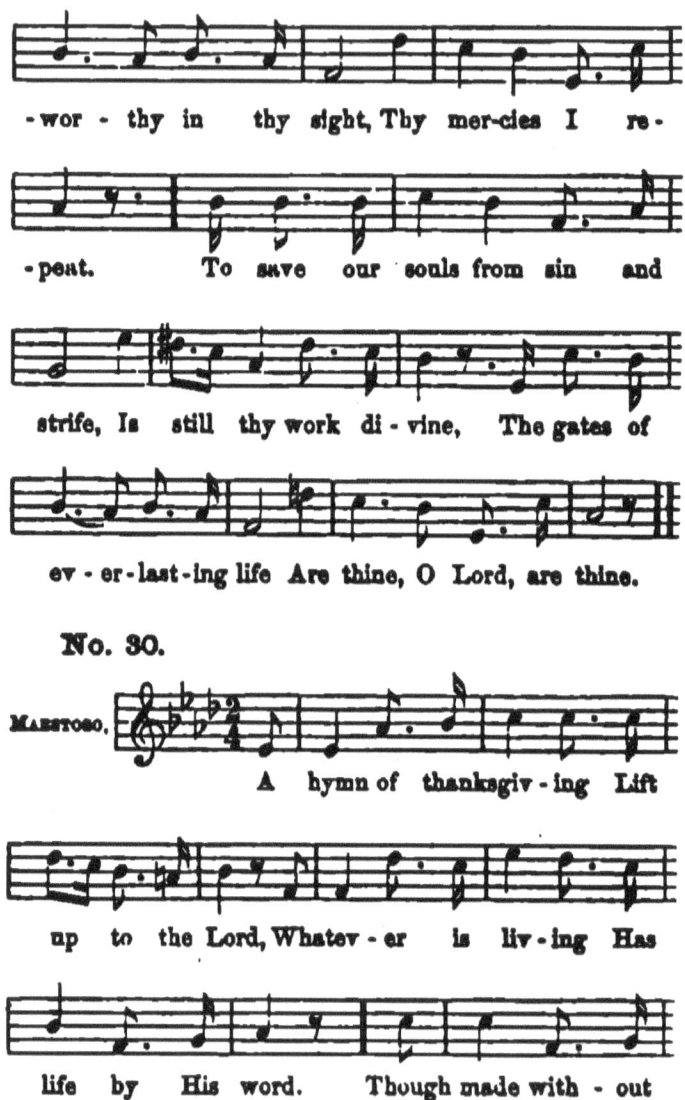

-wor - thy in thy sight, Thy mer-cies I re-peat. To save our souls from sin and strife, Is still thy work di - vine, The gates of ev - er - last - ing life Are thine, O Lord, are thine.

No. 30.

MAESTOSO.

A hymn of thanksgiv - ing Lift up to the Lord, Whatev - er is liv - ing Has life by His word. Though made with - out

30    SONGS FOR CATHOLIC SCHOOLS.

No. 32.

ANDANTE
SOSTENUTO.

What light is streaming from the skies, Re-
-veal-ing heav'n to mor-tal eyes, What
voice is sing-ing from the spheres, An-
-ge-lic hymns to mor-tal ears? O
ho-liest mys-te-ry of love, From
his e-ter-nal throne a-bove, The
Sav-iour comes, un-seen, to dwell A-
-mong the souls he loved so well.

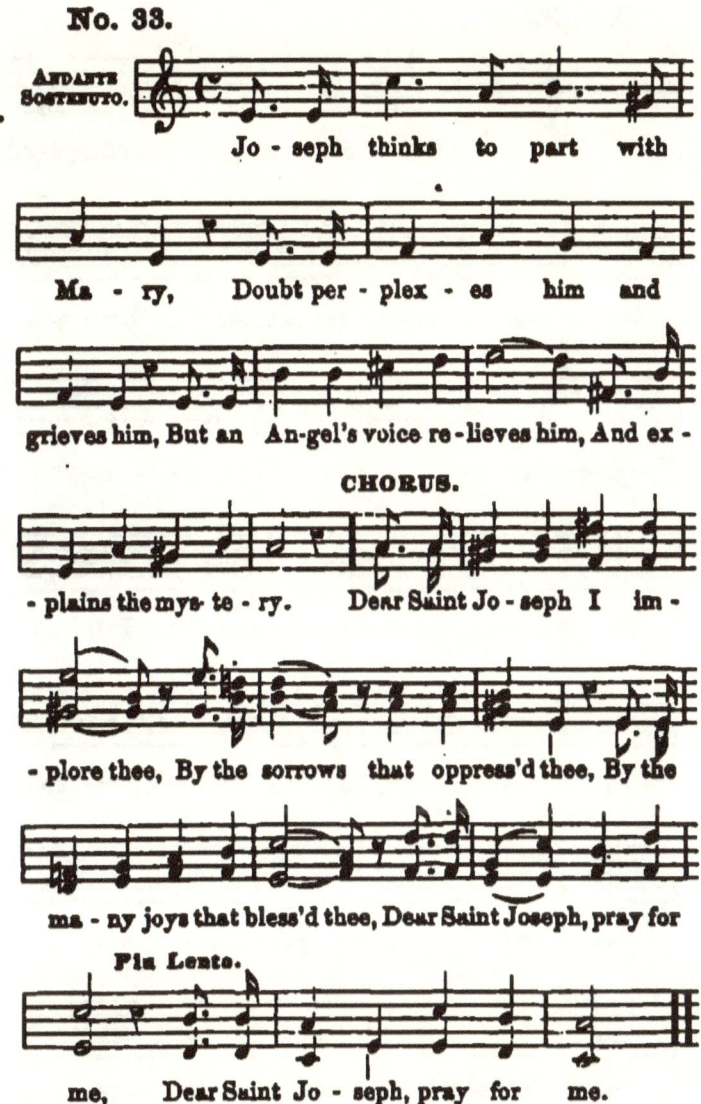

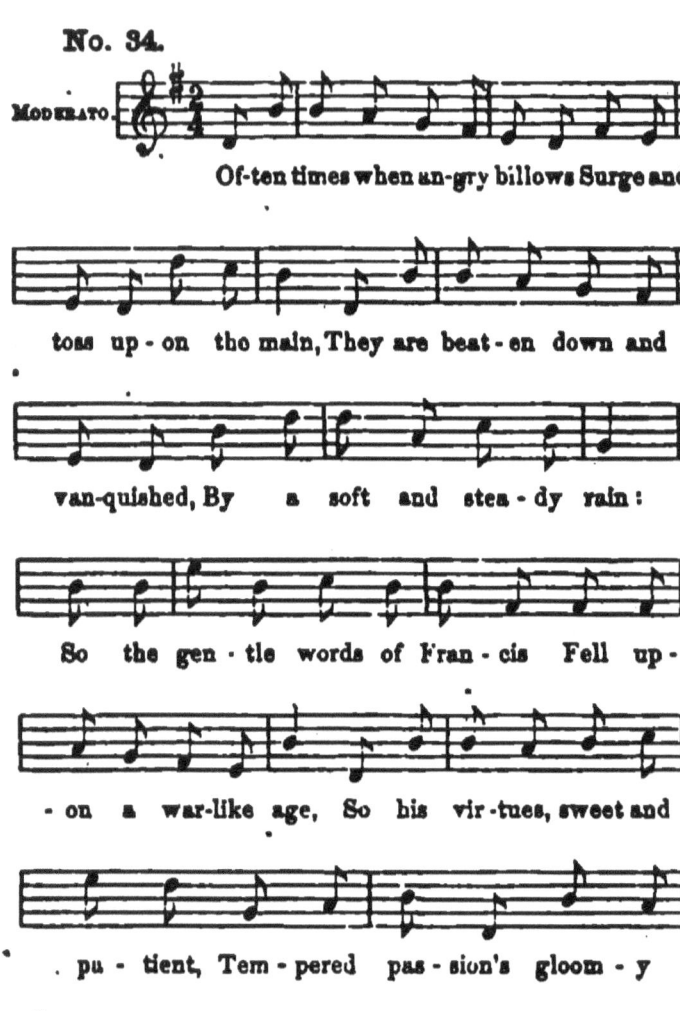

## No. 35.

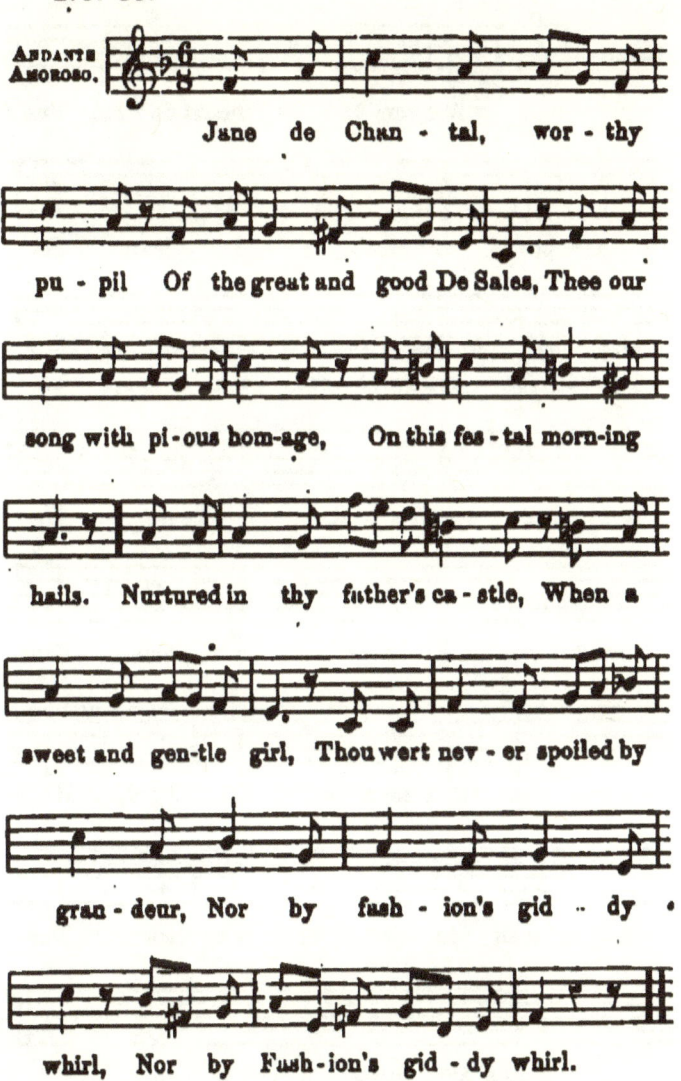

## SONGS FOR CATHOLIC SCHOOLS.

### No. 36.

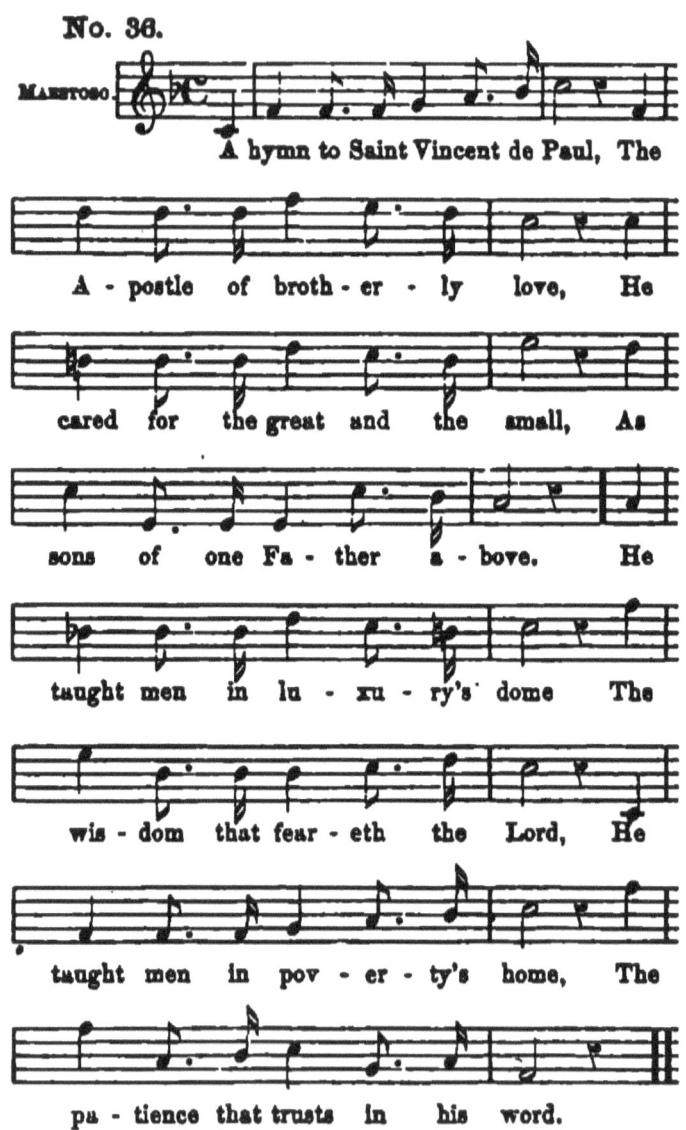

MAESTOSO.

A hymn to Saint Vincent de Paul, The
A - postle of broth - er - ly love, He
cared for the great and the small, As
sons of one Fa - ther a - bove. He
taught men in lu - xu - ry's dome The
wis - dom that fear - eth the Lord, He
taught men in pov - er - ty's home, The
pa - tience that trusts in his word.

# No. 38.

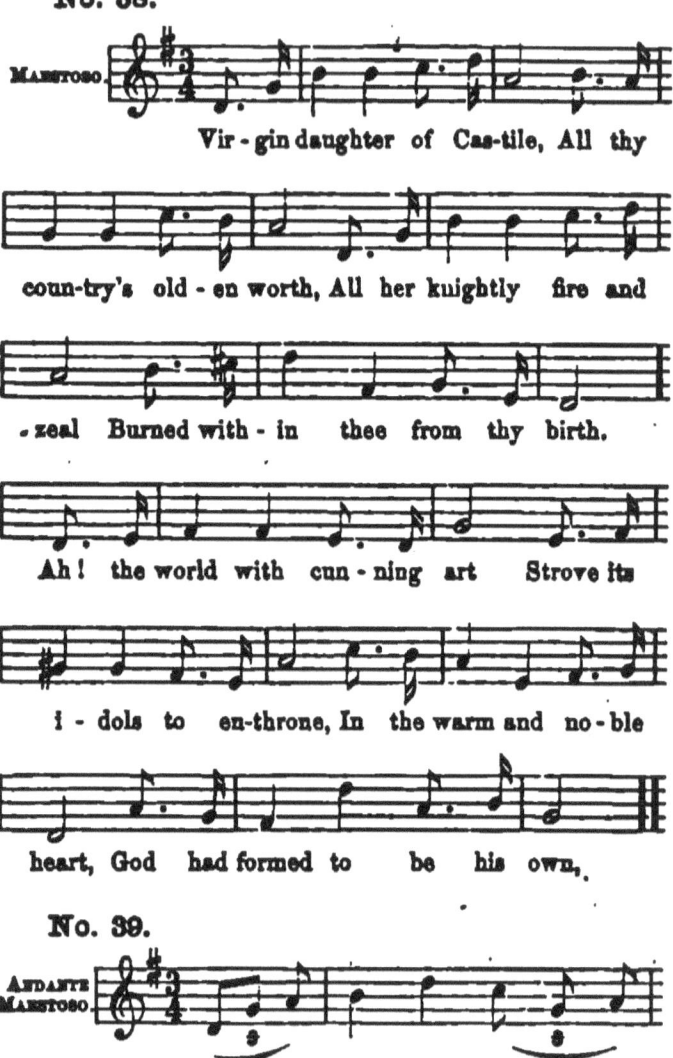

Maestoso.

Vir-gin daughter of Cas-tile, All thy coun-try's old-en worth, All her knightly fire and zeal Burned with-in thee from thy birth. Ah! the world with cun-ning art Strove its i-dols to en-throne, In the warm and no-ble heart, God had formed to be his own.

# No. 39.

Andante Maestoso.

Help of Chris-tians while the

38  SONGS FOR CATHOLIC SCHOOLS.

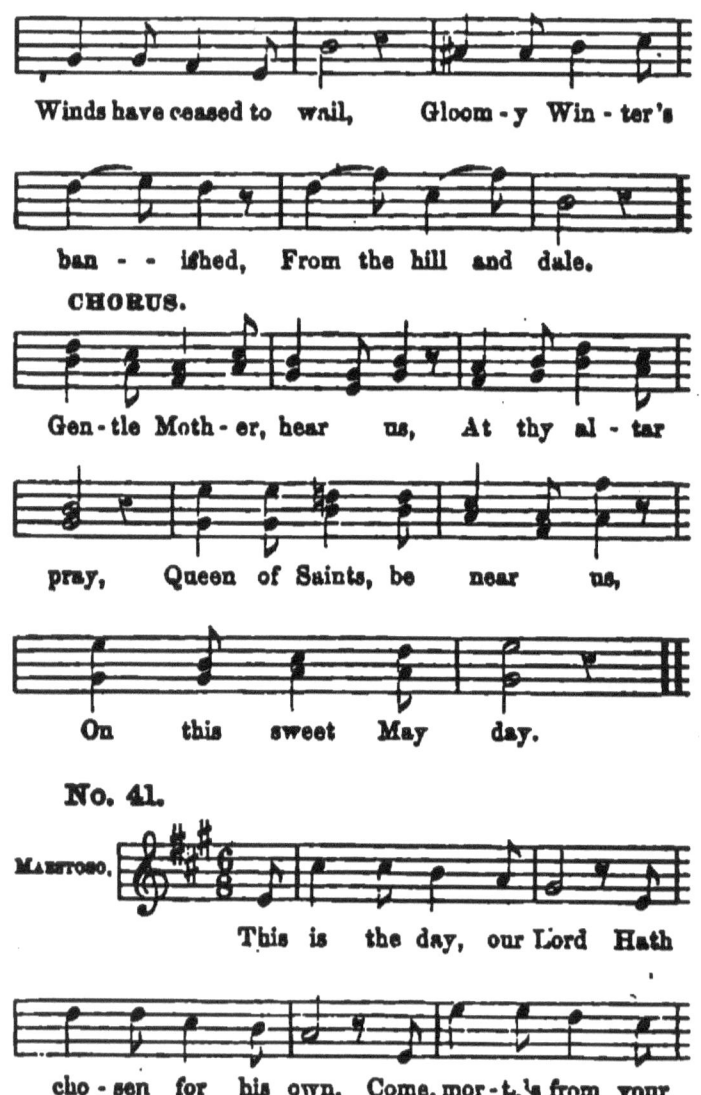

Winds have ceased to wail, Gloom-y Win-ter's ban- - ished, From the hill and dale.

**CHORUS.**

Gen-tle Moth-er, hear us, At thy al-tar pray, Queen of Saints, be near us, On this sweet May day.

**No. 41.**

Maestoso.

This is the day, our Lord hath cho-sen for his own, Come, mor-tals from your

## SONGS FOR CATHOLIC SCHOOLS.

on - ly friends a - round him were The
low - - ly and the poor. Yet
to his Fa - ther's will re - signed, The
new - - born in - - fant smiled; This
came to pass in Beth - le - hem, When
Je - - sus was a child,

**No. 43.**

Andante Maestoso.

There are sev - en bright spir - its that

## No. 46.

I hear a voice from Beth-lehem, The

moan of winds re - sem -bling, It swell - eth up-ward

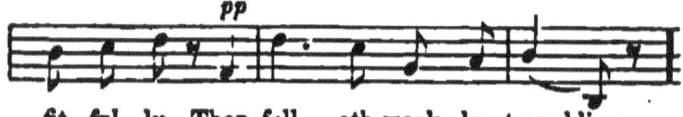

fit - ful - ly, Then fall - eth weak - ly trem-bling.

'Tis Ra - chel, mourn-ing bit - ter - ly, Her

young in cold death sleep-ing, O'er Ra - ma spreadeth

drear-i - ly, The cho - rus of her weep-ing.

## No. 47.

Hear the word Of the Lord.

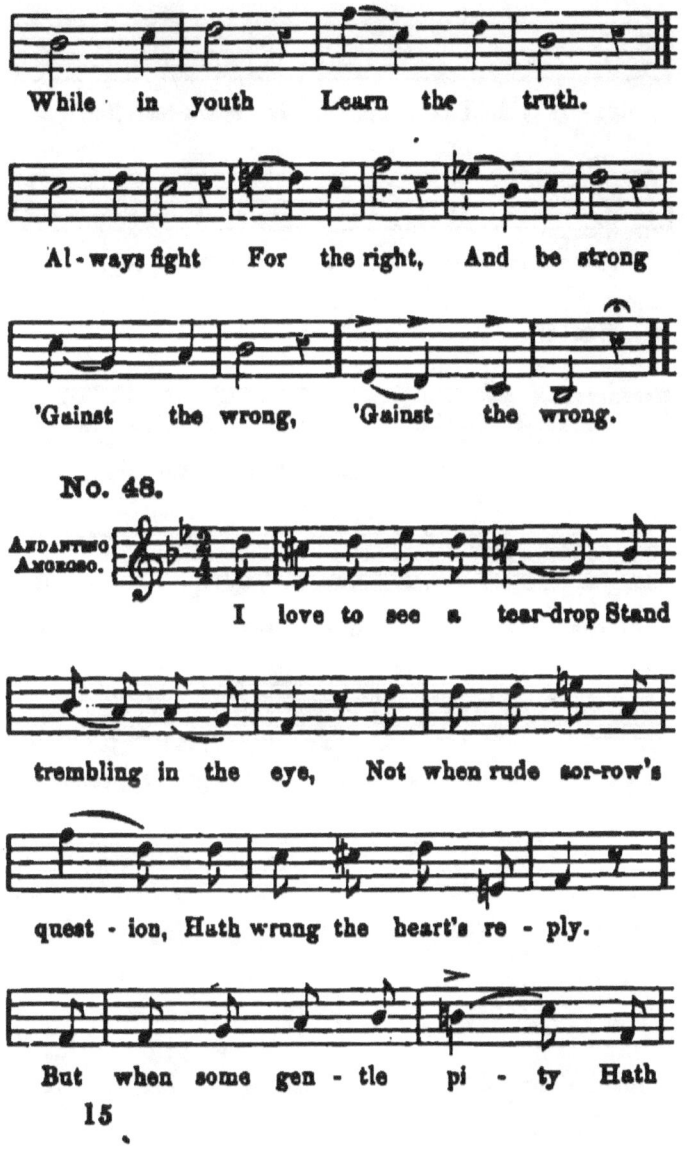

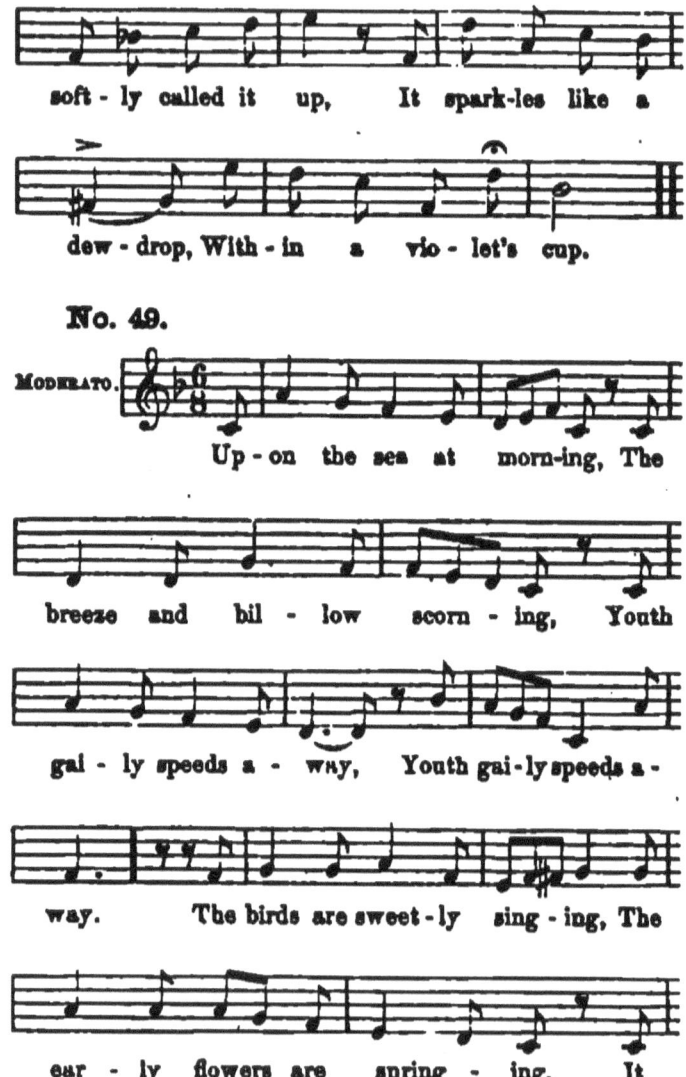

is the dawn of day, It is the dawn of day.

### No. 50.

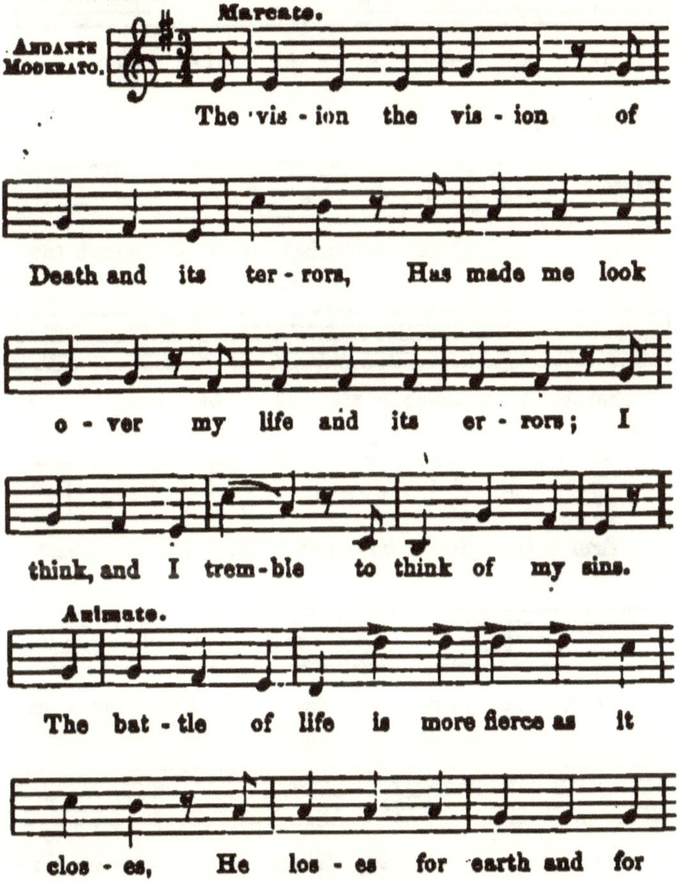

ANDANTE MODERATO. Marcate.

The vis-ion the vis-ion of Death and its ter-rors, Has made me look o-ver my life and its er-rors; I think, and I trem-ble to think of my sins.

Animate.

The bat-tle of life is more fierce as it clos-es, He los-es for earth and for

care is to pre-pare, Her heart for sor-row's

CHORUS.

sword. Moth-er! our sins with sev-en

swords, Have pierced thy sa-cred breast, But in thy

pre-sence and the Lord's, All sin we now de-test.

No. 54.

ANDAN-
TINO.
The Son of God came down from

heaven, Up-on the earth to dwell; And

man con-demns to cru-el death. The

SONGS FOR CATHOLIC SCHOOLS. 51

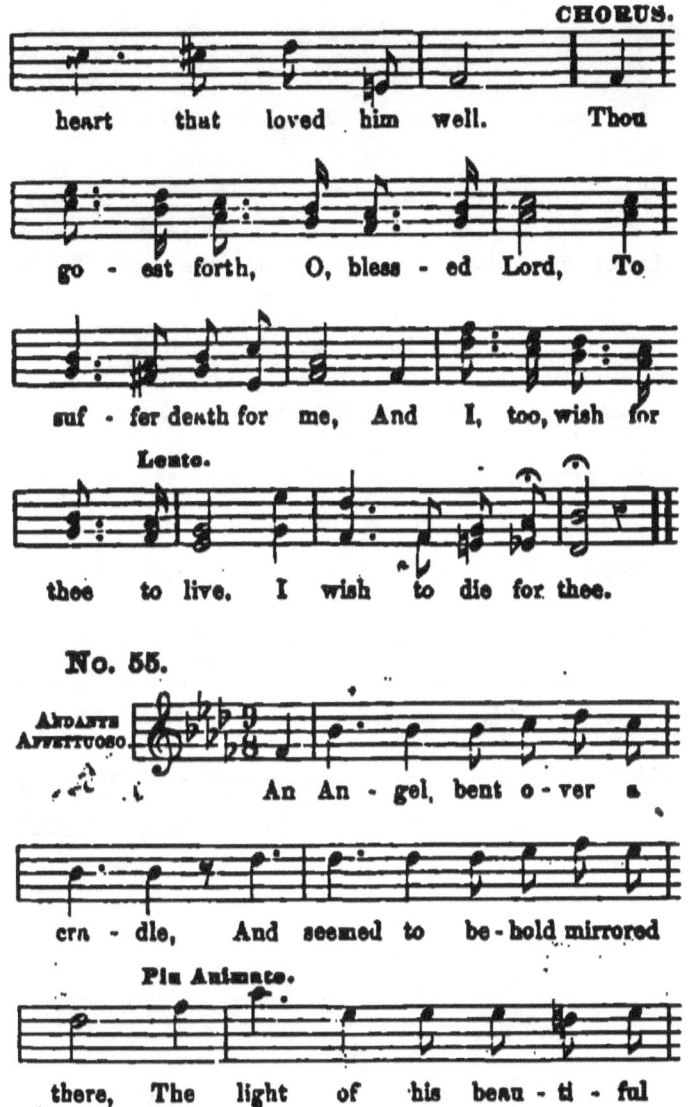

CHORUS.

heart that loved him well. Thou go - est forth, O, bless - ed Lord, To suf - fer death for me, And I, too, wish for

*Lento.*

thee to live. I wish to die for thee.

No. 55.

*Andante Affettuoso.*

An An - gel bent o - ver a cra - dle, And seemed to be - hold mirrored

*Più Animato.*

there, The light of his beau - ti - ful

## 54 SONGS FOR CATHOLIC SCHOOLS.

**No. 57.**

ANDANTE SOSTENUTO. *pp* Una sola voce basso.

It is the hour, it is the hour of prayer, For-get the earth, for-get all earth-ly care.

Alcune voci Soprano.

Be - fore the Lord of heav'n and earth bow down With sim - ple hearts, and wor-ship at his throne, With sim - ple

Rall.

hearts, and wor-ship at his throne.

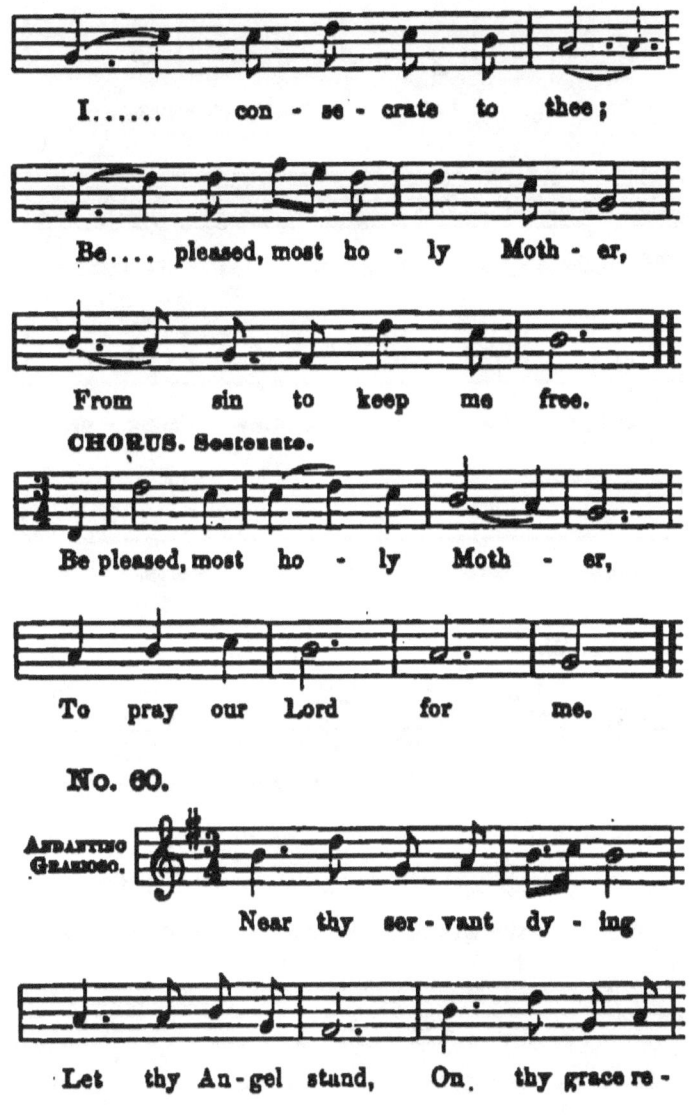

I...... con - se - crate to thee;

Be.... pleased, most ho - ly Moth - er,

From sin to keep me free.

**CHORUS. Sostenuto.**

Be pleased, most ho - ly Moth - er,

To pray our Lord for me.

**No. 60.**

ANDANTINO GRAZIOSO.

Near thy ser - vant dy - ing

Let thy An - gel stand, On thy grace re -

58 SONGS FOR CATHOLIC SCHOOLS.

-ly - ing, Let my heart ex - pand.

When these eyes no long - er See the light of

earth, Let my faith grow strong - er,

Shine with bright - er worth.

No. 61.

Andante Sostenuto.

Pun - ish me not in the

day of thy wrath, Strike me not sud - den - ly

down on my path; Let not the en - e - my

SONGS FOR CATHOLIC SCHOOLS. 59

laugh at my fall, Pi - ty me, Lord, who hast

pi - ty for all. Judge of the fa - ther - less,

hope of the weak: Re - fuge and help of the

low - ly and meek, Look on my wretch-ed - ness,

list to my grief, Turn for thy mer - cy's sake.

grant me re - - lief.

No. 62.

Maestoso.

Yes, I have heard that whis - per,

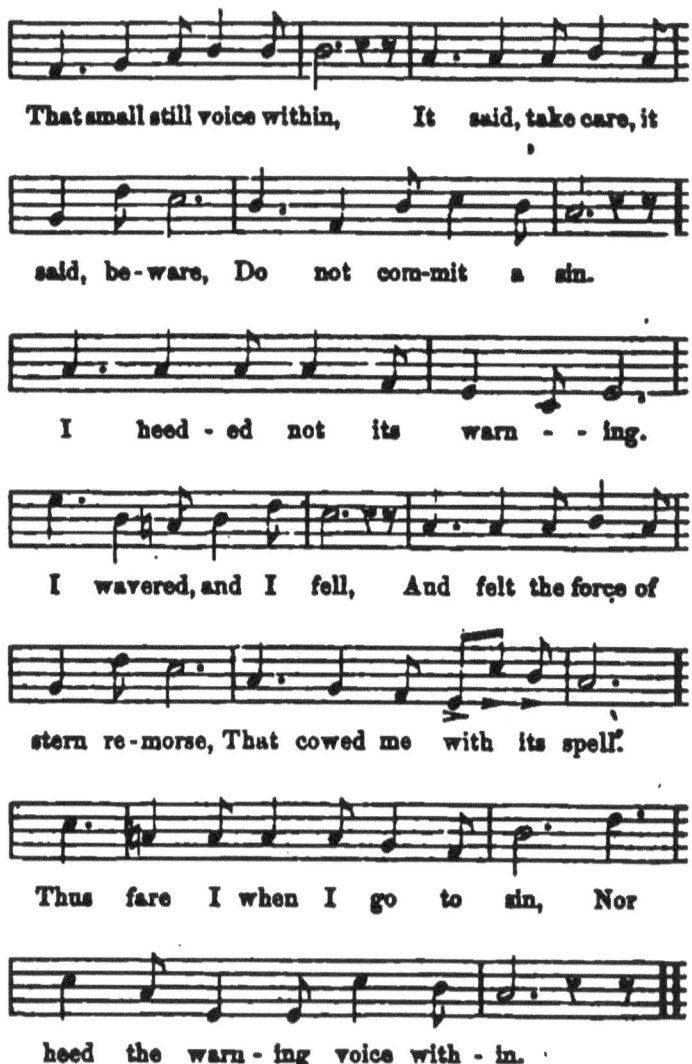

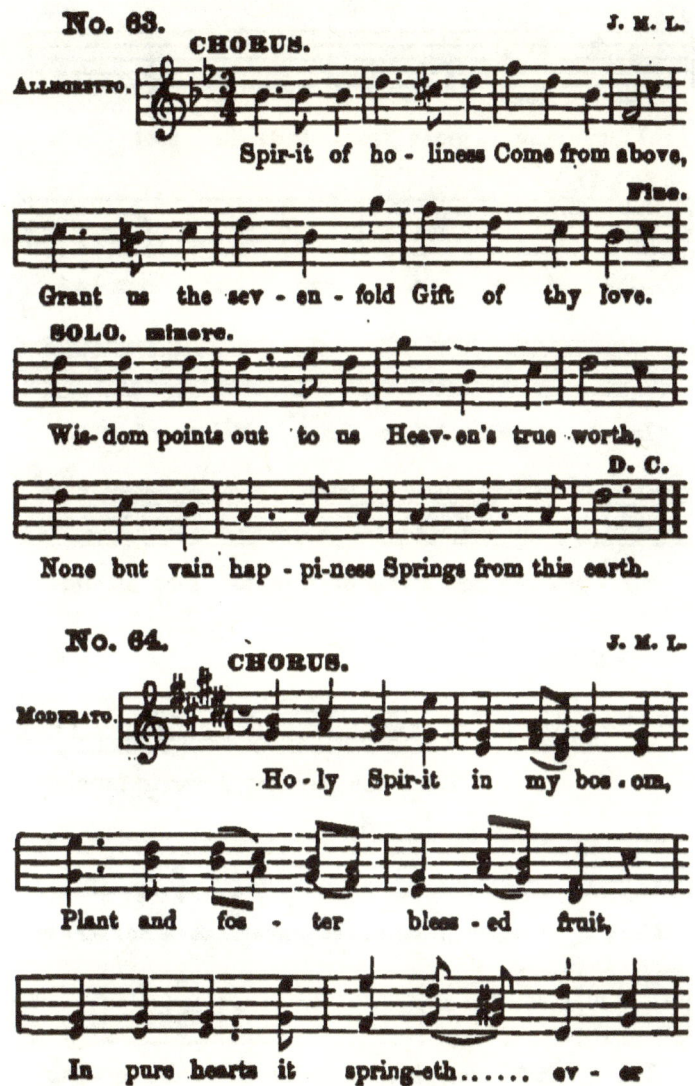

62   SONGS FOR CATHOLIC SCHOOLS.

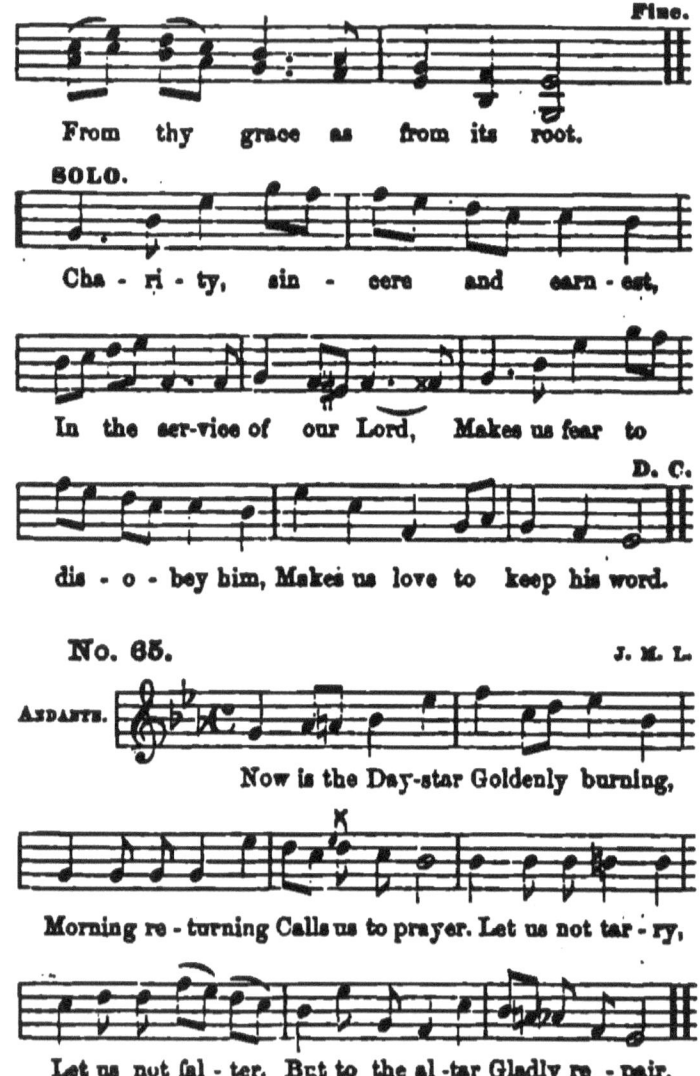

From thy grace as from its root.

**SOLO.**

Cha - ri - ty, sin - cere and earn - est,

In the ser-vice of our Lord, Makes us fear to

dis - o - bey him, Makes us love to keep his word.

No. 65.                                      J. M. L.

**ANDANTE.**

Now is the Day-star Goldenly burning,

Morning re - turning Calls us to prayer. Let us not tar - ry,

Let us not fal - ter, But to the al -tar Gladly re - pair.

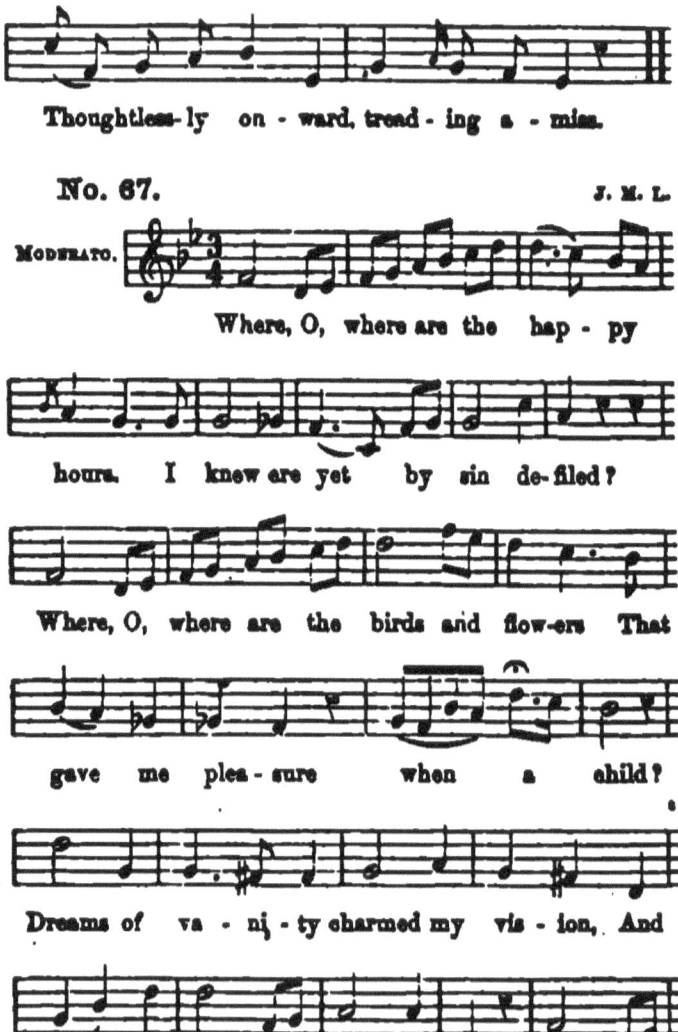

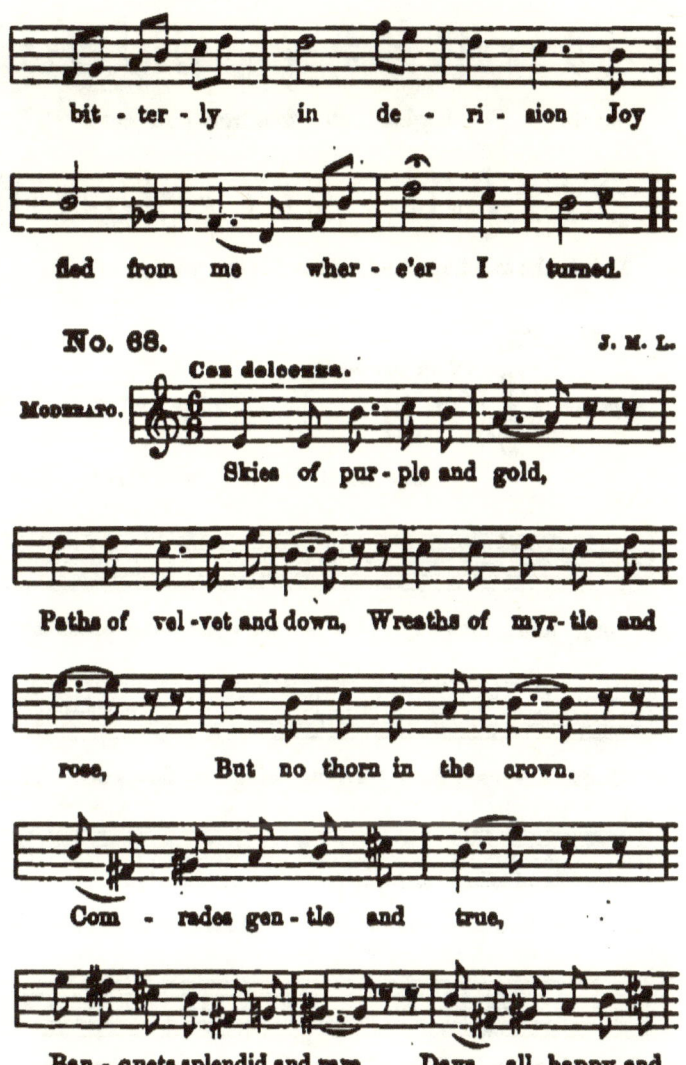

66    SONGS FOR CATHOLIC SCHOOLS.

bright,      Nights  all   free from dull  care,

This is the tale hope told, When life was young, not old.

### No. 69.                                J. M. L.

MODERATO.   Con espressione.

My heart is  sad  and hea-vy, The

long and lone-ly hours De-part-ing pluck no

thorn a-way, Re-turn-ing bring no flow-ers. The

clouds are frowning 'round me, The light is fainter growing, And

friendship's voice I hear it now, Not caring or not knowing.

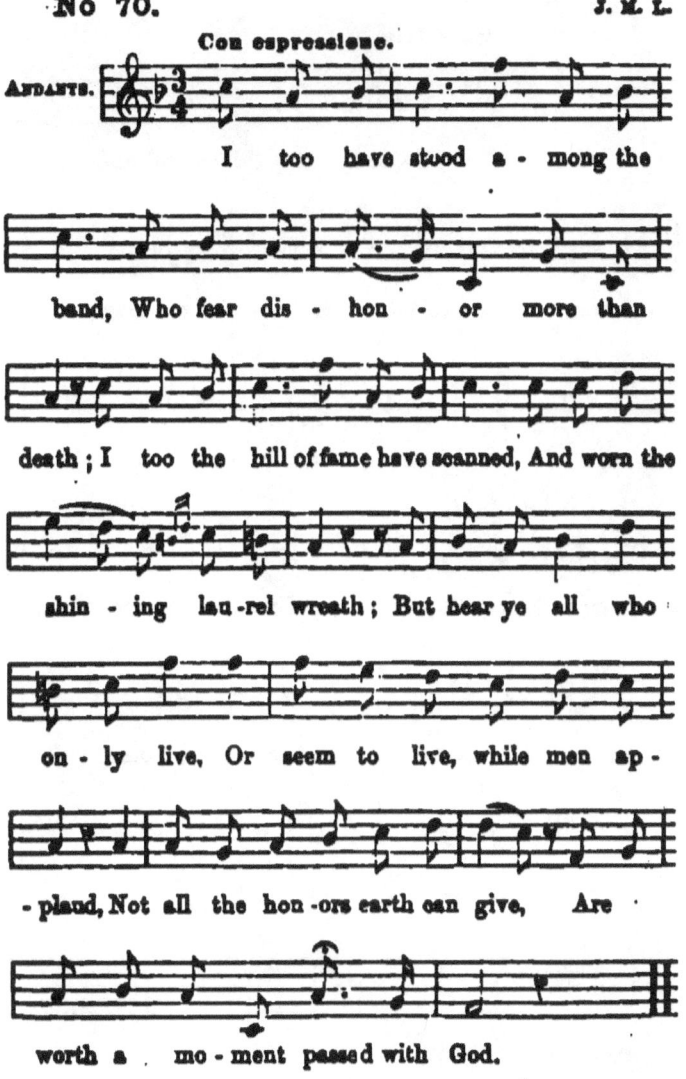

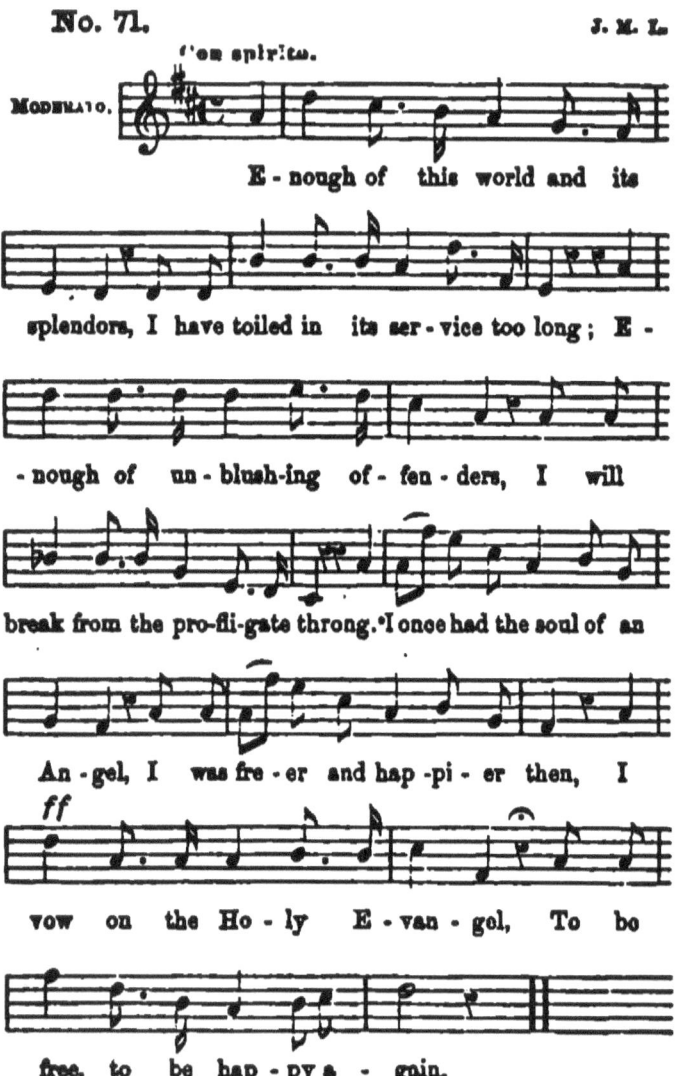

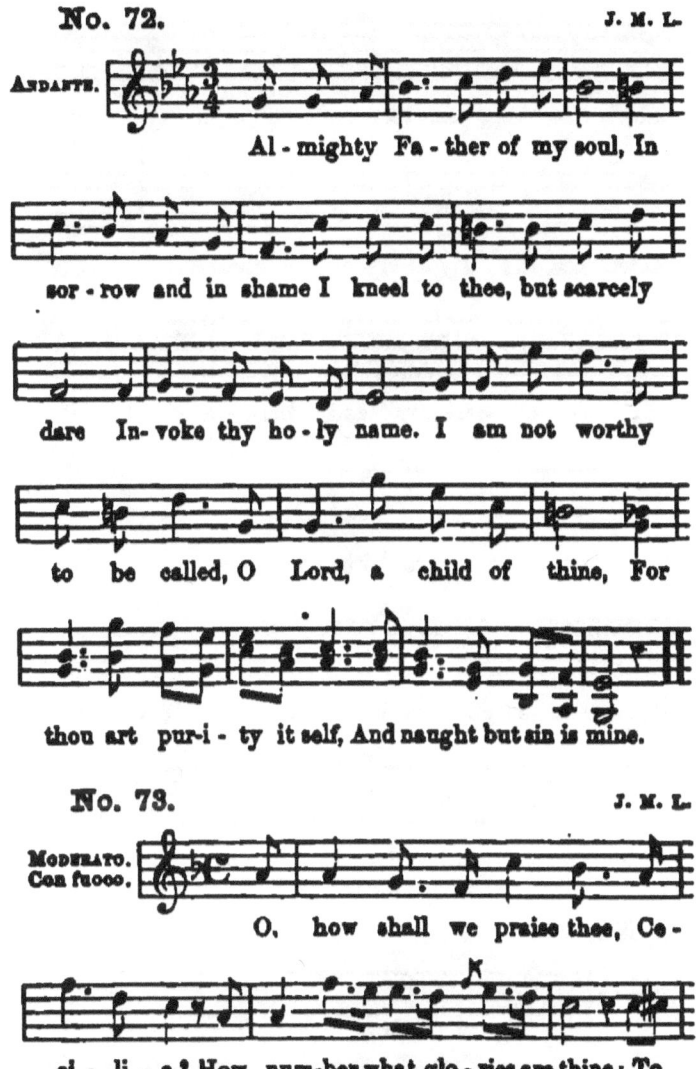

70  SONGS FOR CATHOLIC SCHOOLS.

crown thee twin em- blems of vic - to - ry, The

palm and the li - ly com - bine.   O,

La - dy, all queen-ly and beau - ti - ful, Our

souls are in love with thy worth, Look

down from thy glo - ry in Pa - ra - dise, And

smile on thy chil - dren of earth.

### No. 74.
J. M. L.

MARTIALE.

First off'-ring of A - me - ri - ca On

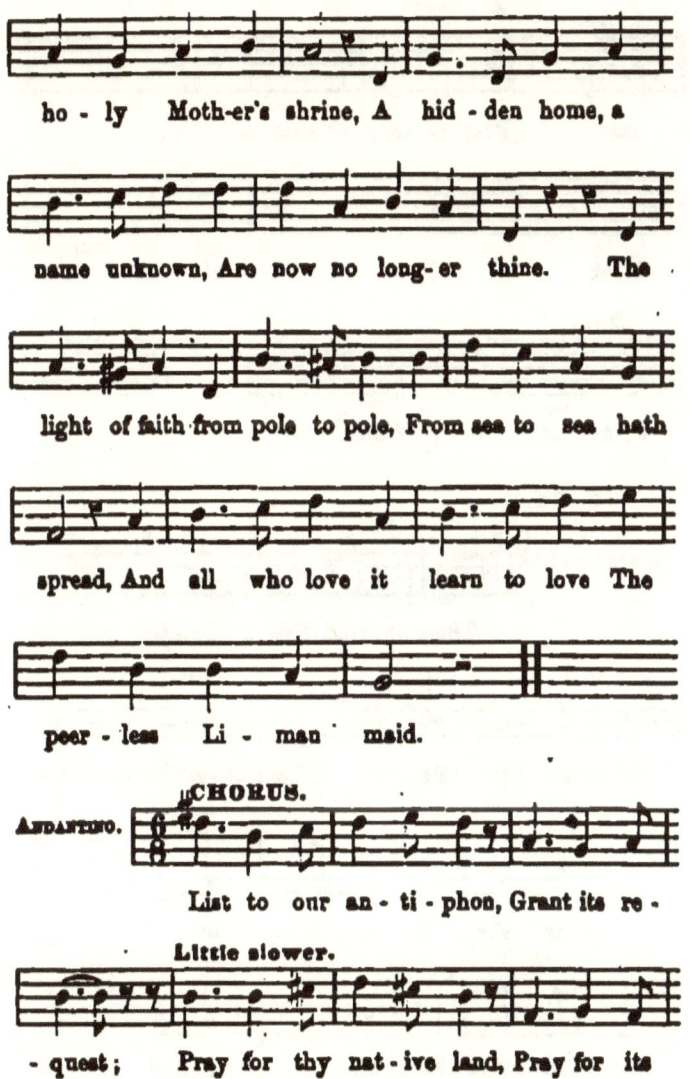

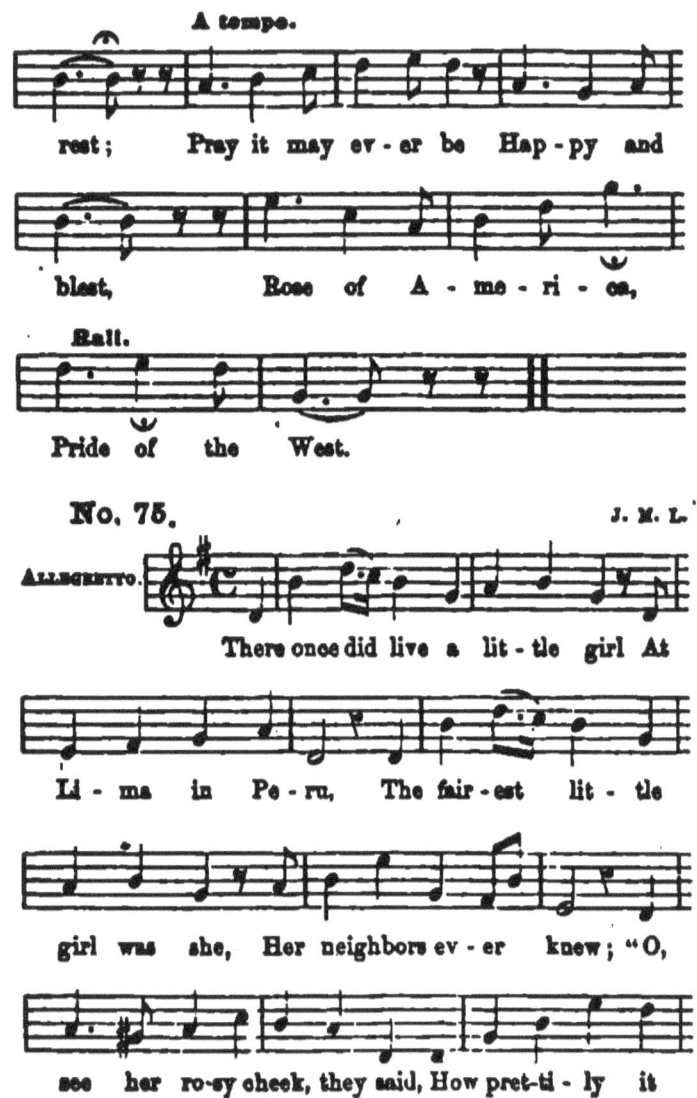

## No. 77.

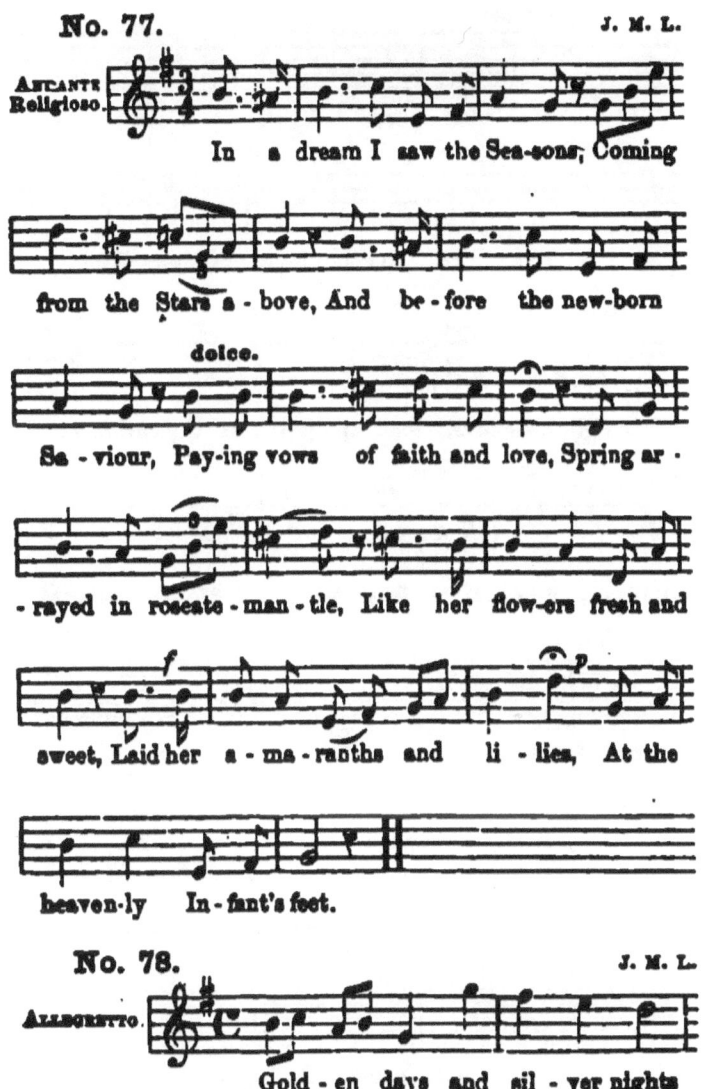

In a dream I saw the Sea-sons, Coming from the Stars a-bove, And be-fore the new-born dolce. Sa-viour, Pay-ing vows of faith and love, Spring ar--rayed in roseate-man-tle, Like her flow-ers fresh and sweet, Laid her a-ma-ranths and li-lies, At the heaven-ly In-fant's feet.

## No. 78.

Gold-en days and sil-ver nights

Fill the soul with pure de-lights, We are hap-py, let us sing, To the moth-er, of our King.

**CHORUS.**

Vir-gin hear our fond ap-peal, At thy shrine we hum-bly kneel, Hear us praise thee ev'-ry day, In the lovely month of May.

### No. 79.

J. M. L.

ANDANTE.

Where the ho-ly Al - tar stands, Un-seen An-gels come in bands, Bear-ing

SONGS FOR CATHOLIC SCHOOLS. 79

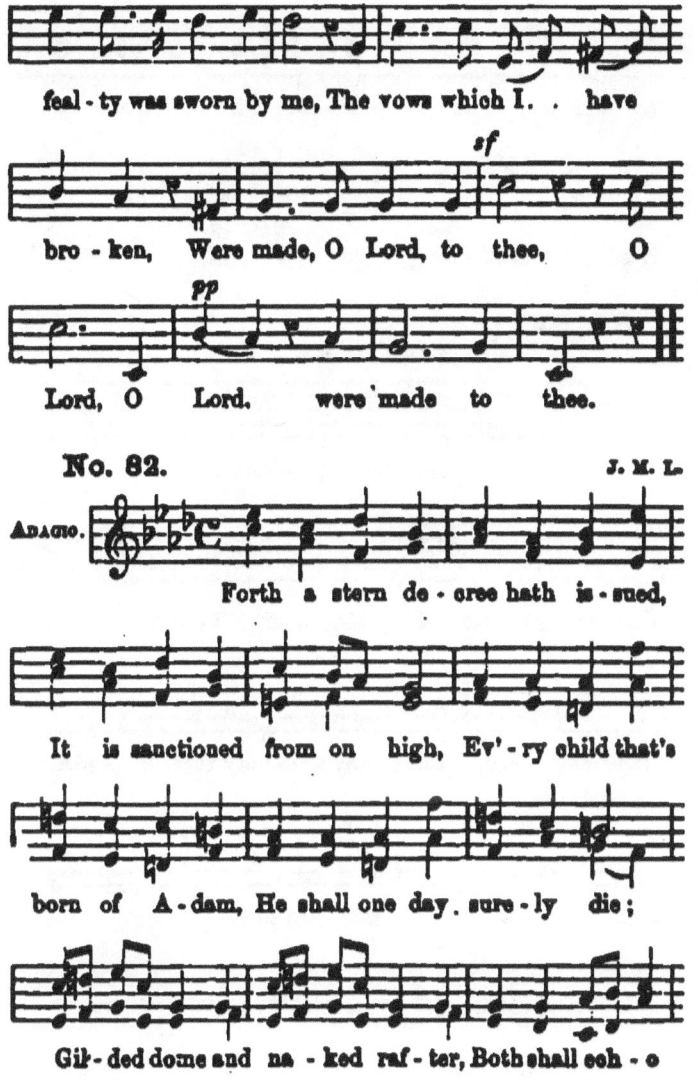

feal - ty was sworn by me, The vows which I . . have

bro - ken, Were made, O Lord, to thee, O

Lord, O Lord, were made to thee.

No. 82. J. M. L.

ADAGIO.

Forth a stern de - cree hath is - sued,

It is sanctioned from on high, Ev' - ry child that's

born of A - dam, He shall one day . sure - ly die;

Gil - ded dome and na - ked raf - ter, Both shall ech - o

80    SONGS FOR CATHOLIC SCHOOLS.

to the call, The Here-af - ter, The Here-af - ter,

We are hast' - ning to it all.

### No. 83.                                   J. M. L.
SOLO. Con dolcezza.
ANDANTE.

Let a pi - ous pray'r be said

For the spir - its of the dead; That their suf-fer-

- ings may cease, That they soon may rest in peace.
CHORUS.

Hear us, Fa-ther, while we pray   For   our

friends now pass'd a - way,   Show them mer - cy,

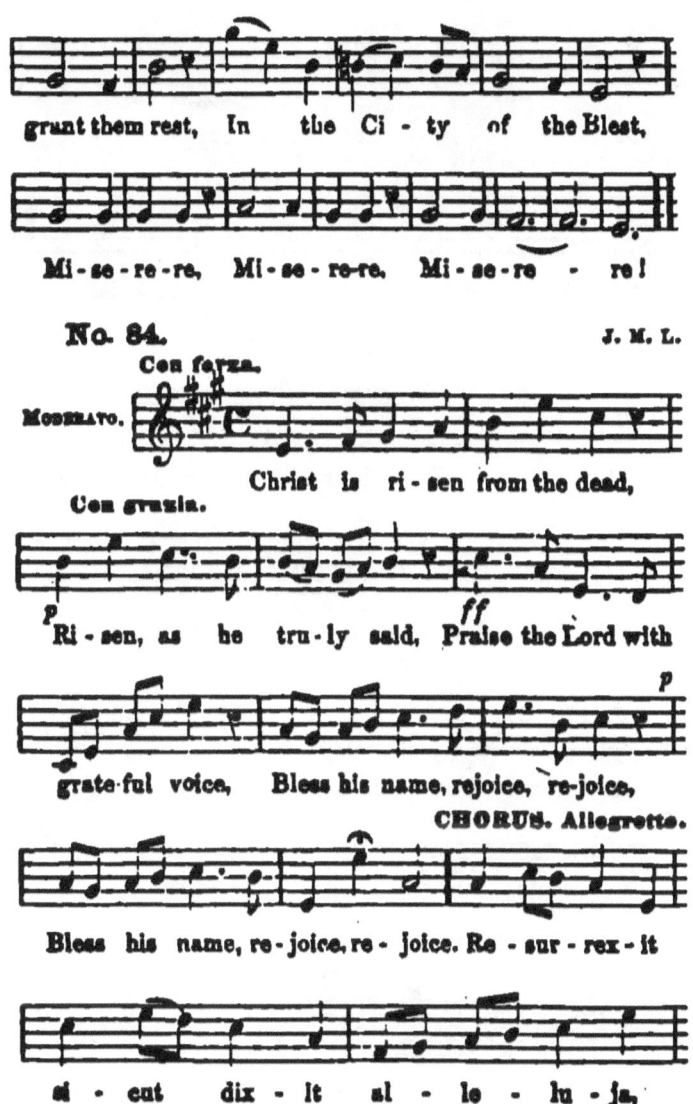

82          SONGS FOR CATHOLIC SCHOOLS.

al - le - lu - ja. Re - sur - rex - it

si - cut dix - it al - le - - - lu - ja.

No. 85.                                        J. M. L.
ANDANTINO.

Zea - lous for the hon - or

Of the Lord a - bove,      May I serve the

do - nor    For his gifts of   love;

Give not earthly pleasure,     Rich- es or re -

- nown,     Give  me for my treasure,

Lord, thy-self a-lone, Give me for my treas-ure, Lord, thy-self a-lone, O Lord, O Lord, O Lord thyself a-lone.

### No. 86.                                   J. M. L.

ADAGIO.

I passed a rose at ear-ly morn, 'Twas blooming fresh and fair, When ev'ning came, a na-ked thorn Was all that met me there, And then my spir-it spoke to me, And thus to me did

84  SONGS FOR CATHOLIC SCHOOLS.

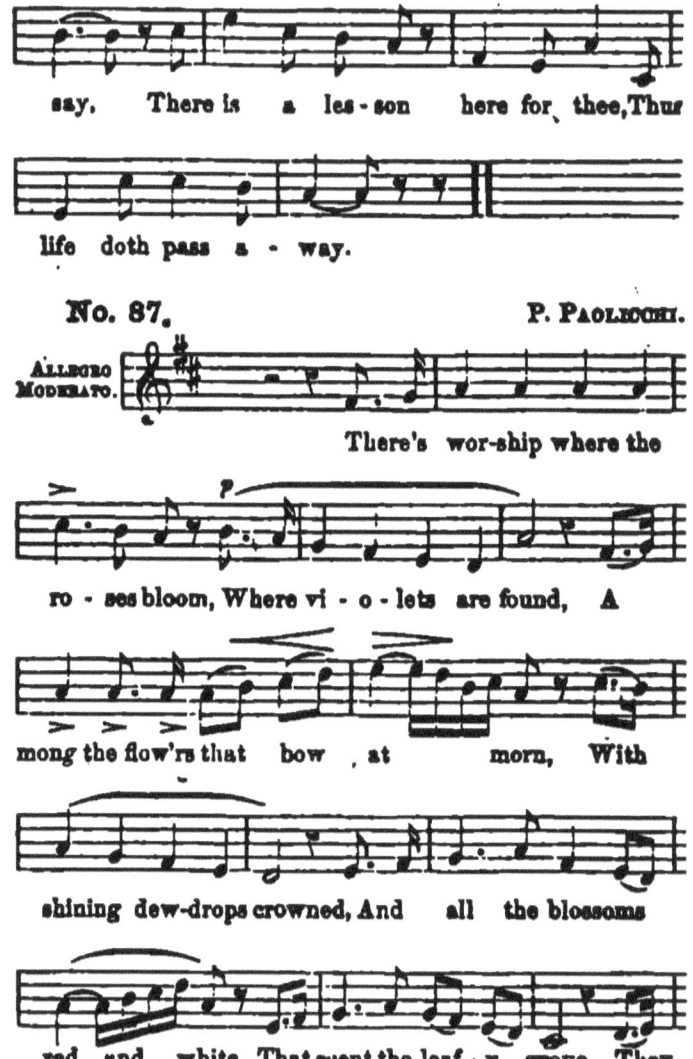

say, There is a les-son here for thee, Thus life doth pass a-way.

### No. 87.
P. PAOLICCHI.

ALLEGRO MODERATO.

There's wor-ship where the ro-ses bloom, Where vi-o-lets are found, A-mong the flow'rs that bow at morn, With shining dew-drops crowned, And all the blossoms red and white, That scent the leaf-y grove, They

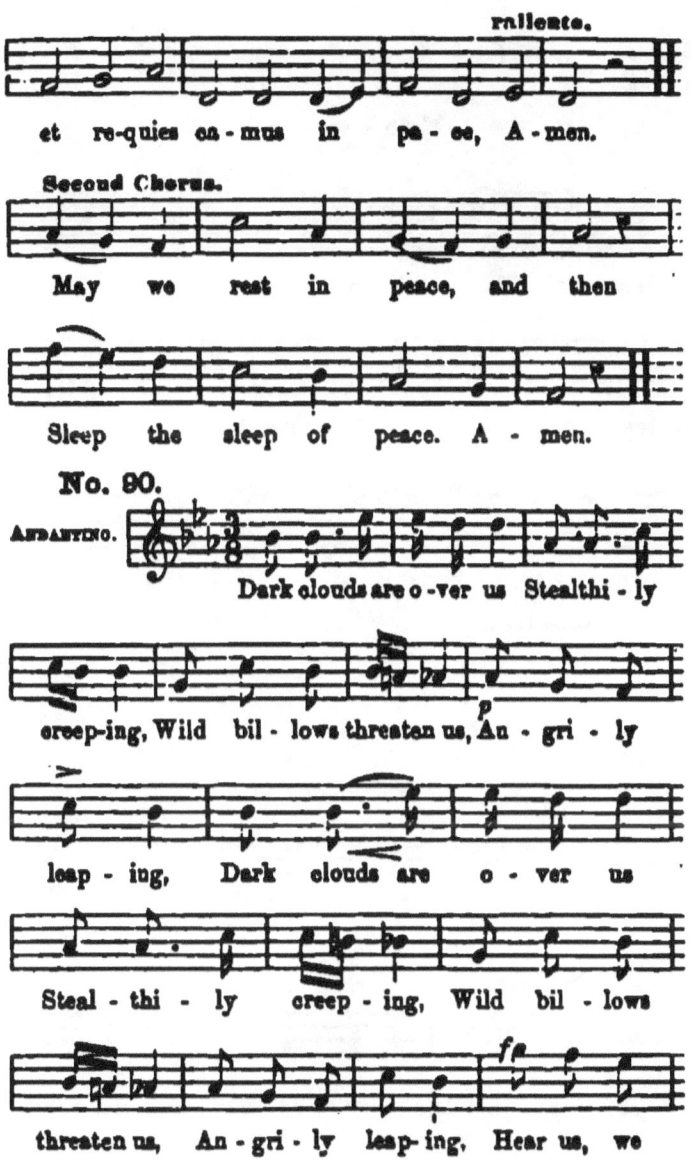

SONGS FOR CATHOLIC SCHOOLS.   89

van-ish,   Let  each  one his  mi - se - ry

ban-ish,   And   be   like the day bright and

fair.    Pour   out  your  full hearts  in   a

cho-rus,    A   cho-rus  of  in - no - cent

glad-ness;   A - way with all  sor-row and

sad-ness,   A - way with all trouble and  care.

No. 92.  RONDINELLA.
ALLEGRETTO.

Twi - light   is    a   witch-ing

www.ingramcontent.com/pod-product-compliance
Lightning Source LLC
Chambersburg PA
CBHW032008230426
43672CB00010B/2296